A Handbook
of Financial
Mathematics

Peter C. Cartledge

Euromoney Books

Published by
Euromoney Publications PLC
Nestor House, Playhouse Yard
London EC4V 5EX

Typeset in 11/13 Times Monophoto Lasercomp by Bath Typesetting Ltd., Bath
Printed in Great Britain by St Edmundsbury Press, Bury St Edmunds

Contents

V Mathematics of short futures contracts and FRAs

VI The arithmetic of equities and linked instruments

Acknowledgements

I am indebted to all my colleagues in the market place over the years whose enthusiasm for knowledge inspired me to take up the noble art of pedagogy. Their advice, support and friendship have enabled me to complete this book.

I am particularly grateful to Nick Goulding who originally inspired me to write the work.

Finally, I am very grateful to Ian Major, who spared me the time for his painstaking advice and help while at a turning point in his own career.

Peter C. Cartledge
August 1991

The Author

Peter C. Cartledge runs his own independent treasury training consultancy, Sigma Associates, following a career with Midland Montagu, the investment and international banking division of the Midland Bank Group.

From 1985, he was Head of Midland Montagu Treasury and Capital Markets Training with responsibility for Midland Montagu's dealers, account managers and support staff throughout Midland Bank Group worldwide, in treasury and capital market skills. Before his departure from Midland Montagu, he was Senior Manager, Treasury Skills Consultancy, in the bank's Financial Engineering Group, where as a Technical Treasury Consultant he designed and ran a comprehensive external treasury training programme for clients.

Peter Cartledge's earlier career included a period of seven years in corporate foreign exchange dealing and in-depth experience in international trade and export finance. He is a member of the faculty of Euromoney Training, and has extensive experience of running seminars in the United Kingdom, Continental Europe, North America and Africa. Publications include a major contribution to *The Foreign Exchange Manual* edited by Rudi Weissweiler.

To Marguerite, Louise and James

1 Starting up

1 Introduction

This handbook has been designed as a user-friendly self-teach course, to allow a wide range of users to proceed at their own individual pace, learning the principles and practice in a structured, progressive way. There is much myth, misunderstanding and even apprehension about the subject of financial mathematics, but in reality it is only applied arithmetic. This approach should therefore allow the relatively non-mathematical reader to come to the subject without feeling that he or she is seriously disadvantaged by the lack of a degree in mathematics.

After a brief introduction to the main tool, an industry standard bond calculator, the handbook starts with simple interest, and through a series of practical and gradual steps, leads the reader to more and more complex concepts. The idea of explaining the theory by using a bond calculator as far as possible, allows the reasonably numerate reader to achieve results without needing to commit too many formulae to memory as would be the case if a conventional, simple calculator was used. To calculate a bond yield using a simple calculator would take so long that interest and precious enthusiasm would soon be lost. In some of the more specialist product arithmetic, in Swaps or Foreign Exchange for example, it will be necessary to show formulae, but the procedures are helped by being able to chain the stages together, one after the other, until the result is achieved.

Following this principle, the handbook provides the reader with many of the theoretical principles to begin with. This is only a means to an end however so that the user may then be aware of what is happening when a given key is pressed. In this way the subject of financial mathematics can be learned much more constructively using a bond calculator.

The objective of the book is therefore to make the reader much more aware of the mathematical implications of many day-to-day treasury and capital market operations. In doing so, it aims to increase financial literacy.

In later sections, such as the chapters covering the mathematics of particular products and product areas—Swaps, or Foreign Exchange or Forward Rate Agreements—a minimum of product knowledge will obviously be required, to understand the purpose of the calculations. An outline description of the product is given, along with examples of how they are priced and used, to enable the reader to proceed with the arithmetic principles. These chapters are not, however, designed to be an exhaustive guide to the products themselves.

1.1 Learning method

The theoretical principles are covered in some detail and the various formulae are set out where this will lead to a greater understanding of the way in which a particular solution is reached. The non-mathematical reader should not be put off by formulae—they are only symbolic "calculators" written down on paper and require working through steadily, substituting numbers for symbols.

The committing to memory of large numbers of formulae is not necessary for greater awareness and understanding. It is however likely to be of use in the understanding of a particular principle, if a commonly used simple formula is identifiable as part of a more complex formula. For example the Yield to Discount formula is used time and again as part of larger and more complicated formulae. It is therefore worth remembering, in order to have a better understanding of what is happening.

From a practical point of view, the optimum, but not necessarily the only method of solving a problem will be set out using the Hewlett Packard HP12C Bond Calculator. This is probably the most widely used bond calculator and it is reasonably easy to use with a little practice. For those who are unfamiliar with it, a section on setting up the calculator is included. This is not designed to duplicate the standard handbook that comes with the calculator, but as an integral "get you going" section. Any problem not covered in the section on setting up should be referred to the manufacturer's manual. The strangeness of the so-called "Reverse Polish Notation" of the keyboard (the order in which data is put into the calculator), is soon forgotten. In a short time, you will probably find this order of things and the lack of the necessity to keep pressing the "equals" sign is more efficient. For those who have the HP19 or similar calculators, you will find that the principles learned in the following chapters, will usually translate quite easily into the format required by these machines, even if some of the keystrokes are a little different.

The main text explains the theory and provides worked examples. At the end of each section, further problems are available for practice.

In some topics, there is no ready made, easy route using the internal programming of the calculator. This means that a formula will need to be remembered, or at least a sequence of key strokes which represents the most expeditious way of working through a formula. Even under these circumstances, there are short cuts that can be used to good advantage. Sometimes, it may be found that there is more than just one way of solving a problem. The methods suggested in the following chapters are well tried but not necessarily the only methods.

1.2   Choosing the right level of complexity

The handbook is designed to increase steadily in complexity. For the more informed reader the easier parts (simple interest, for example) may well be thoroughly familiar. The handbook does however demonstrate many relevant uses of the HP12C itself, and even at the more basic level these sections and procedures may be of practical benefit to the more advanced. The advanced reader is therefore recommended not to dismiss these sections without a glance.

1.3   Keystroke awareness

Much of the handbook is calculator intensive; it is therefore essential to try to be aware of the nature of the keystrokes you are using at all times. This requires a good measure of concentration and a mental picture of what information you are keying in and what the result is likely to look like. If your concentration starts to fail, there will be a tendency simply to "press buttons" without thinking, which will not teach you anything. This is the time to stop for a while as you will never remember the key strokes for a complex calculation, without understanding what is going on.

For example, when starting to use the "PV" key, think "this is the value now, or the price or value at the start of a transaction". Later this will become automatic, like using a minus sign on an ordinary calculator.

By progressing through topics relevant to you, you will become familiar with the principles involved. In a financial market's environment it is rarely necessary to remember in detail how a price or yield is calculated. Most of us employed in the industry will have software which will do the job. This does, however, need care. A lack of understanding, leads to the lack of any ability to identify an incorrect result, because it "looks wrong". Such an ability is vital.

Additionally, a lack of understanding of why or how computer software works something out, is guaranteed to place you in an embarrassing position when someone, a client perhaps, asks you to explain what you are doing.

2 Setting up the HP12C

2 Introduction

The following guide briefly identifies what the main keys are used for. If you require more information, this will either appear later in the relevant section or can be obtained from the handbook. It is not intended that this document should be a substitute for the handbook, but merely a quick, "get you going" guide.

2.1 The keyboard

The keyboard is more like a computer than a calculator. The most significant absentee is the "=" sign. The order in which you input information is therefore important. The consequence of this is that ordinary arithmetic follows this pattern:

Number

Enter

Number

Sign

This is so-called Reverse Polish Notation. It is easy to get used to. The main keys and techniques are as follows:

ON

Toggle type, on/off switch. Power on returns calculator to last entry immediately before power off.

f & g

Prefix keys pressed to access alternative key functions in ORANGE and BLUE on the keyboard.

2.2   Clearing the calculator

CLx
Clears the LAST ENTRY only

Clearing functions

Using the orange alternative key notation

f CLEAR PREFIX
Clears incorrect prefix

f CLEAR REG
Clears all registers and display (the "x" register) but leaves programs

f CLEAR FIN
Clears financial registers only. Keys marked n, i, PV, PMT & FV

f CLEAR Σ
Clear statistical registers only. Keys 1 to 6

f CLEAR PRG
Clears programs

2.3   Setting the number of decimal places

Key f and the NUMBER required.

e.g. "f2" sets display to two places.

N.B. Display is rounded, but calculator always calculates with its maximum of nine decimal places. Can be done at any stage in a calculation without disruption.

2.4 Arithmetic functions

The CHS key.

This key will change the sign $+/-$ of the figure in the display (the x register). Use after keying numbers, but before entering them. The sign of interim answers can also be changed, before continuing with a calculation.

Hint

Note the order in which keystrokes are made. This will seem unusual after using ordinary calculators, but can be an advantage when chaining calculations together in formulae. There is of course no " $=$ " sign.

Exercise

(Set to 2 decimal places):

$10,000,000 \times 30/365$

Key f CLEAR REG (clearing fully before a new sequence will be assumed from now on)

Key	Display	
1	1	
EEX	1	00
7	1	07
ENTER	10,000,000	
30	30	
X	300,000,000	
365	365	
÷	821,917.81	

Change the number of decimal places to 4 [f4]

Note

(a) The rounding that took place in the calculation.
(b) The use of the EEX key to save keystrokes.
(c) The order in which the signs are input (after each figure).
(d) The number of decimal places can be changed at any time.

2.5   Storing and recalling numbers

Sometimes it may be useful to store interim answers; however, it is often unnecessary. To input to store key STO and the number of the register.

You require to store the answer to the previous calculation in register 0.

(There are 20 registers; 0 to 9 and .0 to .9.)
(Turn the calculator back on if it has turned off, noting that the previous answer is displayed unchanged.)

Key

STO 0	store number
f CLEAR FIN	clears the financial registers
CLx	clears the display
RCL 0	note that the figure is recalled
f CLEAR REG	clear the entire calculator

If you now try to recall the number by keying RCL 0, you will not be able to do so.

Note

Registers 0 to 9 and .0 to .9 and the Display are intact after using the sequence f CLEAR FIN.

CLx only clears the display (the x entry).

Exercise

Practise storing numbers in the machine and recalling them after clearing the display only.

Alldown Securities plc has four payments to make in two days' time, in dollars but paid for in pounds, at an exchange rate of £/$1.8155 dollars to one pound:

$759,624.32

$524,896.00

$366,500.00

$877,841.03

Now, STOre the exchange rate into register 1 and use it repeatedly, ReCaLling it as required (like a constant) to convert each amount to pounds. Note that recalling it does not change it.

Note

This saves you putting in the same figure four times.

Do not press "ENTER", since there is no need.

We will cover the use of constants later, as this exercise is designed to teach the use of storing and recalling numbers.

2.6 Calendar functions

D.MY & M.DY

Accessed through blue "g" key and digits 4 (D.MY) and 5 (M.DY). Normal European setting is D.MY and sets the date format for calculations. D.MY appears in display. Default is US date format, M.DY.

Set up for European format before proceeding, key g D.MY.

Using DATE and $\triangle$DYS keys.

Problem

You have bought a Short Gilt, the 12 per cent 1994 stock. Settlement is on the 4th February 1991, the last coupon date was 21st December 1990. How many days interest have accrued since last the coupon?

Key	Display	
f CLEAR REG	0.0000	
f6	0.000000	(6 decimal places needed for dates)
21.121990	12.121990	
ENTER	12.121990	
4.021991	4.021991	
g$\triangle$DYS	(then "running" for several seconds) $= = = = >$ 45.000000	

(Thus interest would accrue gross at 12% of principal $\times$ 45/365)

Variation

Now, substitute the gilt edged stock with a Eurobond. These pay interest on the basis of 12 30-day months (including February). This is usually written "30/360 basis" the significance of this will be explained in a later section of the book.

Key	Display
f CLEAR REG	0.000000
21.121990	21.121990
ENTER	21.121990
4.021991	4.021991
g$\triangle$DYS	45.000000
x > < y	43.000000

Thus interest would accrue for 43 days on a Eurobond or AIBD basis (see section 3.2).

Note that this area, which is concerned with interest accrual and day-year basis will be covered in much greater depth at a later stage.

Problem

Let us assume that today is the 24th March 1991. A 90-day bill has been drawn on a Sterling Acceptance facility today and accepted by the drawee bank. When does it mature? (Take into account that maturity must be on a business day and don't forget to clear before you start.)

Key	Display
24.031991	24.031991
ENTER	24.031991
90	90
g DATE	22.06.1991 6

Conclusion

The acceptance matures on the 22nd of June 1991, which is a Saturday. Conventionally this would be paid on the following Monday. (Monday = 1, Tuesday = 2, Sunday 7, etc.) The HP12C will not advise you of public holidays however!

As an interesting little exercise, you could now work out the day of the week on which you were born, by working out how many days you have been alive from birthdate until today (frightening) and then subtracting that number of days from today, using the DATE function. The number on the far right of the display being the day of the week on which you were born. Monday's child is . . . . . . etc!

2.7   Percentages

Uses %T, △% and % keys.

Note the order in which these keys are used. It is critical that from now on the information in the display will not be illustrated, with the exception of the result.

Problem

The premium on a Currency Option to buy dollars against the Deutschmark at an exchange rate of $/DM1.5000, is quoted as 1.55% flat for a given period. What is the dollar cash premium required for an option on DM1,500,000.00 (equivalent $1,000,000)? Tidy up the display by using two decimal places.

Key	Display
1	
EEX	
6	
ENTER	
1.55	
% = = = = >	15,500.00

Problem

What is the interest payable, in a full year (365/365) on a sterling deposit of £2,422,364.98 at a rate of 13% per annum?

Key	Display
2,422,364.98	
ENTER	
13	
% = = = = >	314,907.45

Problem

Your investment in an ordinary share in HP Ltd has grown from 98 pence to 110 pence in a given period, what % growth does this represent?

Key	Display
98	
ENTER	
110	
△% = = = = >	12.24%

14

The percentage change is 12.24% flat.

Problem

Spot $/DM is offered at 1.5135 and the one month (31 days) outright forward is $/DM1.5155 precisely. What is the annualised percentage discount on the Deutschmark?

Key	Display
1.5135	
ENTER	
1.5155	
△ % = = = = >	0.13
31	
÷	
360	
X = = = = >	1.53% p.a.

Problem

Your score in a test is 185 marks out of total possible of 200. What percentage is this?

Key	Display
200	
ENTER	
185	
%T = = = = >	92.50%

Note that the *total* goes in first, the *mark* next.

Problem

You have a 90-day Bill of Exchange for A$670,000 before you. From this an interest payment has been deducted, of A$26,890. What is the annual rate of discount used?

Key	Display
670,000	
ENTER	
26,890	
%T = = = = >	4.01%
90	
÷	
360	
X = = = = >	16.05% p.a.

General note

There is nothing particularly unusual in these keys, but they are often useful in speeding up calculations as they are a single key operation.

2.8 Constants

General note

When using the HP12C, care should be taken not to use the ENTER key more than is necessary in a particular calculation. Pressing it twice enters the displayed number into two different registers, three times enters it into three registers in a stack. This can have repercussions on later calculations. In using constants this multiple keying is actually done deliberately.

Problem

An export receivable worth US$2,525,324.56 is due in 6 months. What is the sterling equivalent at £/$1.6350 SPOT and £/$1.6300 FORWARD respectively?

Key	Display
2,525,324.56	
ENTER	

ENTER

ENTER

1.6350

$\div$ = = = = >   1,544,541.02

R↓ (= = = = >   2,525,324.56)

1.6300

$\div$ = = = = >   1,549,278.87

This will work indefinitely. The 2,525,324.56 is entered into all three registers above the display, when the R↓ is pressed it rolls the registers down, one by one like a continuous loop with the numbers on it.

2.9   Chain calculations

In a chain calculation, several calculations are carried out one after the other, in different stages, but without the need to store interim answers in the calculator manually.

Problem

The cash compensation payable under a Forward Rate Agreement is calculated using the following formula, figures having already been substituted. Work the formula using normal mathematical priorities, without storing or writing down and re-inputting any interim figures. The figures in the formula matter little at this stage, if you are unfamiliar with FRAs. What is important is that you learn the correct approach of working left to right and treating the ENTER key as a bracket function.

Hint

If you are unsure what to do, adopt the following approach:

1. Key the first number, 15,525,000.
2. Ask yourself, "can I do anything with this number?" If the answer is "no", then hit the enter key and pass on to the next number, which is 7.3750, key that into the display.
3. Can you do anything with the 7.3750, the answer is no, so ENTER and move on.

4. Key 6.8750, can you do anything with it? Yes, you can subtract it from the previous number, so hit "−". And so on. It might be better in the early stages of learning, just to work with sections of the formula, writing things down, making for the ultimate conclusion.

$$\frac{[15,525,000 \times (7.3750 - 6.8750) \times 62]}{360 \times 100} \times \frac{1}{\dfrac{[1 + (6.8750 \times 62)]}{360 \times 100}}$$

This time we will bring back the display contents. Set to 4 decimal places.

Key	Display	
15,525,000	15,525,000	
ENTER	15,525,000.00	
7.3750	7.3750	
ENTER	7.3750	
6.8750	6.8750	
−	0.5000	
62	62	
×	31.00	
×	481,275,000.0	
360	360	
÷	1,336,875.000	
100	100	
÷	13,368.7500	(gross figure)
1	1	
ENTER	1.0000	
6.875	6.8750	
ENTER	6.8750	
62	62	
X	426.2500	

18

360	360
÷	1.1840
100	100
÷	0.0118
+	1.0118
1/×	0.9883
X	**13,212.3126**

Conclusion

The fully discounted figure payable is $13,212.31.

Note

(a) The use of the one stroke *reciprocal key* (1/x). It is very useful in all kinds of yield and discount calculations.

(b) The handbook shows that the recommended way of solving such a formula is to start inside the innermost brackets and work outwards, rather than starting from left to right and working top to bottom. This, of course, is a perfectly acceptable way of working with formulae using the HP12C. In the writer's experience, however, you can sometimes lose track of where you are in a complex formula. Users will doubtless perfect their own techniques over time.

II Money and capital markets

3 Simple interest calculations

3.1 Relating to the calculator

3.1.1 Percentage key reminders

The three percentage keys are significant in the calculation of simple interest. This section shows how they can be used to good advantage to avoid using formulae which have to be committed to memory. Most of the time, it will be better to use the proper calculator procedures for the simple interest calculations, rather than the percentage keys.

3.1.2 Cash flow conventions

Sometimes the HP12C requires the signing of cashflows to produce meaningful answers. Any form of cash <u>outflow</u> must therefore be preceded by a <u>minus</u> sign. <u>Inflows</u> are thus <u>positive</u> and a sign is not necessary. In complex calculations directional cash flow analysis will have to be carried out to establish the correct input for the calculator. The text will indicate when to use plus or minus signs.

3.1.3 End of month interest payment

The "END" key.

This is accessed through the blue "g" key. The default setting is END (nothing appears in display). Most interest payments are made at the end of each interest period. There are occasions (annuities due, for example) when we need to consider payment made at the beginning of each interest period. This will be covered in later chapters.

3.2 Day-year calculations

Before any interest calculations can be made, it is essential to grasp fully the variety of day-year conventions which apply to the many different instruments, bills, bonds, deposits etc., on which interest has to be calculated, in a variety of different currencies.

For example, the Eurodollar deposit market (Libor) convention is to use the actual number of days in the period divided by a 360 day year, usually abbreviated to "ACT/360". This means that when calculating accrued deposit interest, the time fraction used will always be the ACTual number of days that interest has accrued, divided by 360.

Example

A time deposit $10,000,000 paying interest at the rate 8.50% p.a., ACT/360.
Placed 12th December 1990.
Matures 12th January 1991.
Annual return: $850,000 (i.e. 10 million × 8.50/100).
Return for period: $850,000 × 31/360 = $73,194.44.

(The calendar function will establish the actual number of days in the deposit period.)

Compare this with the Eurobond market. The convention here is 360/360, or twelve 30 day months in the year. This is usually referred to as the AIBD basis (Association of International Bond Dealers).

Example

Purchase bond for settlement 12th December 1990.
Redemption (repayment) 12th January 1991.
Annualised return [coupon 8.50%, investment $10,000,000 price: par]
= $850,000.

Return for period 850,000 × 30/360 = $70,833.33.

Note
The HP12C calculator will take account of "AIBD basis" when calculating the number of days between two dates.

Using the dates in the two previous examples:

12th December 1990 ------- > 12th January 1991 (use D.MY mode).

Key	Display
12.121990	
ENTER	
12.011991	
g△DYS = = = = >	31

This gives the number of calendar days and is appropriate for bases using the actual number of days as a fraction of the year.

For Eurobonds (amongst others) this is not so, as the basis is 30/360 (or 360/360).

Continue by keying:

$$\times > < y = = = = > \qquad 30$$

This gives the number of days on an AIBD basis, which in this case is 30.

Example

Calculate the number of days between 28th February 1988 and 1st March 1988 on both bases.

Answer	1. 365/360 = 2 days
	2. 360/360 = 3 days

Why?	1. Because 1988 is a leap year
	2. Because there are 30 days in every month including February when using AIBD basis.

These conventions have to be taken into account when comparisons are made between the returns on different instruments. The key is the size of

25

the time fraction, and the assumption that returns on two comparable instruments should be comparable, in cash terms, even though different bases are used.

i.e. a US dollar Time Deposit vs a US dollar Treasury Bond

[365/360]   [Actual/Actual]
8.00% p.a.   8.00% p.a.

The two rates may appear the same but do not represent the same cash return on the investment. One of the reasons for this is the different conventions used in the two markets.

(There may be other reasons such as interest payment frequency, but we will ignore these at present.)

Example

1. \$10,000,000 at 8% = 800,000 × 365/360
                     = 811,111.11 for a full year
2. \$10,000,000 at 8% = 800,000 × 360/360
                     = 800,000.00 for a full year

Thus the time fraction 365/360 produces a larger cash return than 360/360. What we can say therefore is that *nominally* the rates are the same but *effectively* one gives a better rate of return. We now encounter the question of nominal and effective rates. Do not be tempted to refer to "real" rates in this context, since this normally concerns interest rates with inflation numbers stripped out.

We may usually assume that those rates quoted in the market place or on a screen are "nominal" rates. Effective rates are those that reflect the actual rate of return in a year. To compare one rate with another, when they are quoted as nominally the same but on different bases, we will need to modify one or the other, to reflect its actual rate of return.

For example, to compare USMM (US Money Market, semi-annually) with US T-Bond basis when they are both quoted at 8.00%, we can modify either but will choose to modify the T-bond basis:

To do this: Rate × 360/365

8 × 360/365

= 7.890411%

Conclusion, 8% T-bond (365/365) is the same as 7.89% on USMM (365/360) basis.

To prove that 7.890411% USMM equates with 8.00% T-bond basis, re-do the calculation:

1. $10,000,000 at 7.890411 = 789,041.10 × 365/360 = 800,000.00 for a full year.
2. $10,000,000 at 8.000000 = 800,000.00 × 365/365 = 800,000.00 for a full year.

Our final conclusion must be that if we have the free choice to invest in either medium, then at these numbers we will be indifferent (to yield). Bear in mind though that if the USMM rate is quoted higher than 7.89, i.e. at 7.95, it would be better than the T-bond rate, even though *nominally* it is lower.

Conclusion

The whole question of day-year calculations should not be underestimated. Often it is ignored. The difference we have just demonstrated amounts to (8.00–7.89) or 11 basis points. This is within 1 basis point of the bid/offer spread in the average money market transaction, or double the spread on the average interest rate swap. This has to be highly significant, but is only half the story. We will return to the question of simple or nominal rates and effective rates at a later stage, when we also examine the question of interest payment frequency, which can have an even more dramatic effect on rates and prices.

3.3 Summary of formulae

1. To convert 365/360 or Actual/360 to:

    a. 360/360

    b. 365/365

    c. Actual/Actual

USE: Quoted Rate × 365/360 = rate on new basis

2. To convert 360/360 or 365/365 or Actual/Actual (these are, for all intents and purposes the same), to:

   a. 365/360
   b. Actual/360

USE: Quoted Rate × 360/365 = rate on new basis

This is particularly important when arbitrage between two instruments is being considered. Under these circumstances, where profit margins can be relatively small, a failure to take day-year basis into account can lock in a loss, where a profit was otherwise indicated.

3.4   True yields

General note on yields

In financial terms the yield on an asset or liability, can either consist of income or capital growth or a combination of both. Initially, in looking at simple yield we are only concerned with income or capital growth over a single period, which is arguably income anyway.

A simple yield represents the return that an investment pays for each interest period. It also represents the interest cost to a borrower of funds for a given period.

For example the simple yield on a bank deposit, which pays 8% per annum, will be 2% per quarter.

The amount of money payable can be calculated using the simple interest formula:

$$\frac{\text{Principal} \times \text{Interest Rate} \times \text{Days}}{360 \times 100}$$

Note that we have used 360 on the bottom line of the formula. This is correct for a Eurodollar bank deposit, but would have to be amended for other instruments, as explained in the previous section.

Example

$10,000,000 for 182 days at 7.63% per annum, yields:

$$\frac{10,000,000 \times 7.63 \times 182}{360 \times 100}$$

$$= \$385,738.89$$

Using the HP12C however, there are two methods which avoid the working through of a formula:

Example

$10,000,000 for 182 days at 7.63% p.a.

Key	Display
1	
EEX	
7	
ENTER	
7.63	
%	
182	
×	
360	
÷ = = = = >	385,738.89 (rounded to 2 decimal places)

This merely uses one of the percentage keys and is quick to carry out. An alternative method uses a pre-programmed facility in the HP12C, which allows certain other operations to be carried out.

Example

$10,000,000 for 182 days at 7.63%

Key	Display
1	
CHS	
EEX	
7	
PV	
7.63	
i	
182	
n	
f INT = = = = >	385,738.89

The last method, although a little more "key intensive", is the most versatile, because of the way the HP12C operates. The PV, i and n keys are, among others, like "cells" or more correctly, "financial registers". You put numbers in and the machine works with them, time and again until they are removed by clearing the registers (by f CLEAR FIN, see setting up procedures).

This means that individual figures in a calculation can be changed and then reworked ad infinitum. Every time you key in another number into n or i or PV, it automatically replaces the one that was there before and so allows infinite numbers of "what if" exercises to be done.

Example

What happens if the rate worsens by 50 basis points?
i.e. $10,000,000 for 182 days at 7.13%

Key	Display
7.13	
i	
f INT = = = = >	360,461.11

Worked examples

Change the period to 64 days = = = = > 126,755.56

Change the amount to $1,252,362.00 = = = > −15,874.38

Change the rate to 6.32% p.a. = = = = > −14,070.98

Notice that, in failing to change the amount, *complete with minus sign*, we finished with negative cashflows for interest. It is therefore quite important, if we wish to get a strictly correct result, to consider which direction cash is flowing. In a loan, for example, the borrower *receives* cash to start with, (+ve) and *pays* interest (−ve) and *repays* principal.

A further refinement of the HP12C is its ability to switch to 365/365 day-year basis at a single stroke. This allows the calculation of accrued interest on UK Sterling Time Deposits, accrued interest on US T-Bonds, Japan Government bonds etc.

The calculator, being of US origin, calculates US Money Market accrual first and US T-bond next. US T-bond can be used for all sterling accrual calculations.

Using the previous example once again but on a UK Money Market basis for sterling:

Example

£10,000,000 for 182 days at 7.63%

Key	Display
1	
CHS	
EEX	
7	
PV	
7.63	
i	
182	

n

f INT $=$ $=$ $=$ $=$ $>$ 385,738.89 (as before)

R↓

X $>$ $<$ Y $=$ $=$ $=$ $=$ $>$ 380,454.79

This is easily proved using the longhand simple interest formula, and the two different time fractions 182/360 (USMMY) and 182/365 (UKMM).

Thus with two additional key strokes the equivalent in 365/365 basis can be calculated.

Manually, if you multiply 385,738.89 by 360/365 you achieve the same result thus also proving the day-year conversion factor.

Final note

The Recall function can be used with the n, i, PV, PMT and FV keys, as well as the storage registers we looked at earlier. If you wished to check what data you had input into perhaps PV, then RCL PV will show you −10,000,000.00 at the moment. Equally, what days did you use? RCL n shows 182, and so on. An important point to observe here is that, once again, looking at the data in these "cells" does not modify it in any way. It is just like opening a pigeon-hole door, looking at what's inside and closing the door again, leaving the contents untouched.

3.5   True discounts

A lender of funds can charge the borrower interest on a principal sum in two ways, either at the end of the loan period, calculating the sum due using the simple interest formula as explained in the previous section, or alternatively, the lender can advance a sum to the borrower, but deduct interest before doing so. In other words, the borrower pays the interest at the front end of the loan.

Example

The holder of an asset, like a Bill of Exchange due to mature in 6 months requires cash today rather than waiting until the Bill matures. The face value of the Bill is $100,000.00 and the interest quoted will be 10% and charged at the front end.

The Bill is *discounted* and the bank lends to the holder a cash payment of:

$$\$100,000 - (10/100 \times 180/360) = \$95,000$$

When the Bill matures, the drawee of the Bill pays new holder (the bank) the full face value of $100,000.00.

Thus with a true discount rate, an annualised percentage number, modified for the number of days, can be deducted from the face value at maturity.

The US Treasury Bill market, the Commercial Paper Market and the Bankers Acceptance Market are all markets where rates are often quoted as true discount rates. The simple interest formula can be used to calculate the amount of interest to be deducted.

Using the HP12C in this context is more complicated than using it for true yields.

Worked example

Calculate the <u>amount of interest to be deducted</u> from a banker's acceptance value $5,000,000 due to mature in 92 days. The discount rate is 7.52%.

Key	Display
5	
EEX	
6	
ENTER	
7.52	
%	
92	
X	
360	
÷ = = = = >	96,088.89

This method uses one of the percentage keys and requires the use of a time fraction.

A better method is to use the PV, i and n keys as with true yields:

Key	Display
5	
EEX	
6	
PV	
92	
n	
7.52	
i	
f INT = = = = >	96,088.89

This method does away with time fractions as the number of days is input into the "n" key. This procedure is, of course, identical to the procedure for true yields in the previous section.

Note also that for a 365 day basis the keystrokes

R↓

x < > y = = = = >   94,772.60

can be added.

We can keep on chaining calculations together, it does not disturb the original calculation. Provided you have not disturbed the calculator:

Key	Display
f INT = = = = >	96,088.89 reappears

Say that as well as knowing how much interest will need to be deducted, you would like to know what the amount will be after deduction. That is how much you will advance.

Key	Display
RCL PV = = = = >	5,000,000
+ = = = = >	4,903,911.11

You have added negative interest flow to positive borrowing receipt, you receive a net sum of $4,903,911.11.

Even at this stage, you can solve again for f INT, the n, i, and PV keys remain undisturbed by your later calculations.

Conclusion

With true yields we can add the quoted percentage to the principal amount. With true discounts, we can subtract the percentage from the principal amount.

3.6   Present and accumulated values

Using simple discounts and yields

CARE

The terms *Present Value* and *Accumulated Value* are abbreviated to "PV" and "FV" in mathematical (actuarial) formulae, in accordance with most conventions. The use of PV and FV in a formula does not necessarily mean automatically that those keys on the HP12C are used.

Introduction

In simple interest discounts and yields, we are not concerned with the reinvestment of interest earned. This question of compounding will be covered in later chapters.

A periodic interest rate is the rate that is charged for a given interest period, i.e. 10% p.a. is 2.50% for a quarterly period. While we do not wish to descend into the welter of formulae which often form an integral part of any work on financial mathematics, or more strictly arithmetic, it will be worthwhile including a few here and there. When discussing the use of periodic rates in financial calculation, a basic knowledge of how the formulae operate will help our use of the HP12C, particularly when we come to compound interest rate arithmetic.

3.6.1   Present values from true discounts

The present value of a sum is, among other things, the principal part only of a total sum repaid together with interest at maturity.

The formula used to calculate this when the rate is quoted as a true discount is quite straightforward:

$$PV = FV \left[1 - ((n \times i)/100)\right]$$

where

PV = Present Value
FV = Future Value
i = periodic interest rate
n = number of interest periods

Substituting

The present value of £5,000,000 bill discounted at 10% p.a. over two and a half years at simple interest, will be:

$$PV = 5,000,000 \left[1 - (2.50 \times 10/100)\right]$$
$$= 5,000,000 \times 0.75$$
$$= £3,750,000$$

A more satisfactory formula can be written as follows:

$$PV = FV \left[1 - ((\text{Days/Basis}) \times (i/100))\right]$$
$$(\text{where } i = \text{discount rate})$$

Worked example

Calculate the present value of a Bill of Exchange for £1,500,000 due to mature in 31 days, discounted at a discount rate of 8.125% p.a.

Substituting in the formula above:

$$PV = 1,500,000\,[1 - (31/365 \times 8.125/100)]$$
$$= 1,500,000 \times 0.993099$$
$$= 1,489,648.97$$

Using the HP12C and another worked example, these calculations can be done as follows.

Worked example

30 per cent of US debt is in Treasury Bills; these are non interest-bearing and are sold at a discount to par (100%). Thus investor income is the difference between the discounted value and par value. All bidding for these instruments is done in terms of a discount rate, on the basis of actual days/360, i.e. US Money Market basis.

A three-month bill of 92 days tenor is bid at 7.25%
What price is payable (% of par value of 100%)?

N.B. The formula is as before:

$$PV = FV\,[1 - ((Days/Basis) \times (Discount/100))]$$

But note: The accumulated value (100%) is entered in the PV key.

Key	Display
100	
PV	
92	
n	
7.25	
i	
f INT	
$-$ = = = = >	98.1472

This means that for every $100 dollars of bills, you pay 98 dollars 15 cents. All you have now done is to calculate the simple interest in periodic percentage terms and subtracted it from 100%.

Thus you can use the HP12C to price US Treasury Bills off the quoted discount rate.

3.6.2   Accumulated values from true yields

The accumulated value of a sum is the total value of principal and interest together at maturity. The following formula will give the accumulated value from an initial, or Present Value.

$$FV = PV(1 + [(n \times i)/100])$$

where

i = the periodic yield

n = number of periods

PV = initial principal sum

FV = accumulated value

What will be the value of 10,000,000 at 10% p.a., simple interest after four years?

Substituting

$$FV = 10,000,000 (1 + [4 \times 10/100])$$
$$= 14,000,000$$

This growth is linear.

We can therefore establish the growth after 2 years 3 months as follows:

$$FV = 10,000,000 (1 + [2.25 \times 10/100])$$
$$= 12,250,000$$

Linking this with the simple interest calculations earlier we have a more comprehensive formula:

$$FV = PV (1 + [(Days/Basis) \times (i/100)])$$

Worked example

Calculate the value of £10,000,000.00 at 7.63% p.a. after 182 days.

Substituting

$$FV = 10,000,000 \ (1 + [182/365 \times 7.63/100])$$
$$= £10,380,454.79$$

Using the HP12C, and a further worked example, these calculations can then be worked using the keys n, i, PV, and FV. We need no formula at all.

Worked example

Calculate the value of $10,000,000 at 8.48% p.a. after 7 days.

Key	Display
1	
CHS	
EEX	
7	
PV	
7	
n	
8.48	
i	
f INT	
+ = = = = >	10,016,488.89

Note

This is the same procedure as the simple interest calculation, but with the addition of the " + " key at the end.

Exercise: try this but with sterling, on a 365/365 day basis.

$$= = = = > \ 10,016,263.01$$

An alternative way of carrying out the calculations above makes better use of the n, i, PV and FV keys.

Worked example

Calculate the value of $10,000,000 at 8.48% p.a. after seven days. This time, you will need to work out the fraction of a year represented by seven days. On a US Money Market basis this is:

$$7/360 = 0.019444$$

Make sure you use enough decimal places, otherwise inaccuracies will creep in, then key:

Key	Display
Key	**Display**
7	
Enter	
360	
÷	
n	
8.48	
i	
10,000,000	
CHS	
PV	
FV = = = = >	10,016,488.89

Adjusting for sterling UKMM, just alter the 7/360 to 7/365.

Important note concerning the "n" key and the HP12C

When using the HP12C, it is safe to use the "n" key as set out above, that is for non-integer numbers, *provided they are less than one*. You should note, however, that it is not safe to use the key for non-integer numbers greater than one, including those produced by such time fractions as 363 days/360, which produce a number greater than one, even though it is less than one financial year. In this case, use the f INT sequence covered earlier; that is quite safe.

This can be proved as follows:

Take a Time Deposit for $1,000,000 at 10% p.a. (USMM Act/360) for 361 days. What will it be worth at the end of the period?

We know that in 360 days it will be worth $1,100,000 exactly, all we then do is add on one further day's simple interest, which is:

$$\frac{1 \times 10.00 \times 1,000,000}{360 \times 100}$$

$$= \$277.78$$

Thus in 361 days it will be worth $1,100,277.78.

If we use the n, i, PV and FV sequence, we get a different result:

Key	Display
361	
Enter	
360	
÷	
n	
10	
i	
1,000,000	
PV	
FV = = = = >	−1,100,305.56

This is not correct, but rather dangerously, looks about right.

To explore this problem further requires a good knowledge of compound interest, and we will look at this later.

3.6.3 Present values from true yields

So far, we have covered present value calculations using true discounts and accumulated values using true yields.

The next stage looks at calculating present values given yields (as distinct from discounts) and accumulated values given a discounted amount (as distinct from yields).

To recap briefly, the two formulae we have used so far are:

1. $FV = PV(1 + [(Days/Basis) \times (Yield/100)])$
2. $PV = FV(1 - [(Days/Basis) \times (Discount/100)])$

Yield versus discount

It is worthwhile at this point to clarify the nature of the yield and the discount.

Basically, the "yield" *works forwards*. An investment (or loan) accumulates value depending on rate of yield, as time passes.

T0   T180

>   >   >   >   >   >

Principal   Principal + Interest

As for the "discount", this *works backwards* from a fixed future value at maturity, to a value today, which depends on the rate of discount.

T0   T180

<   <   <   <   <   <

Principal − Interest   Principal

Referring back to the two formulae in the introduction to this part, note the following inflexible rule which we will continue to apply:

When using a true **YIELD** rate, use a **PLUS** sign in the formula
(i.e. *plus* is synonymous with *accumulating* forwards)

When using a true **DISCOUNT** rate use a **MINUS** sign in the formula
(i.e. *minus* is synonymous with discounting or *reduction* back)

42

There are many occasions when we wish to discount an amount to its present value, but we only have the yield rate quoted. For example, all money market rates are quoted as true yields. Using yields, (rates of forward growth), we now know how to calculate an accumulated future figure from a starting one. Since most rates of interest and return are quoted in the market place and on screen as yields, what happens if we wish to calculate a value today, knowing what the end value is and a rate of yield.

Problem

We have an obligation to deliver a fixed amount of £1,500,000 to a client in 182 days. If we buy sterling, how much do we need to invest TODAY at a money market yield of 8.125% p.a. to give us £1,500,000 in 182 days time?

Before embarking on solving this problem it is worth looking at some more basic principles:

Information: Rate 10%

Amount 100

Period 1 year

1. Used as a yield:
    Borrow 100 repay 110 (interest = 10)

2. Used as a discount, with interest subtracted from 100
    Borrow 90 repay 100 (interest = 10)

In both cases, interest is 10 units but the true cost of funds is quite different.

In example 1 the true return is £10 on £100 or 10%
In example 2 the true return is £10 on £90 or 11.11%

Thus discount of 10% p.a. gives a true yield of 11.11% p.a. In other words, you cannot discount amounts by deducting the percentage yield.

As a guide you may always assume that the corresponding yield is always higher than the true discount.

Thus in our example we cannot just deduct the appropriate portion of 8.125% because that would give a yield much higher than 8.125% p.a.

As observed in an earlier formula, all the ones that use quoted yield have a "plus" sign in them.

Our third of the four main formulae is no different.

$$PV = FV \left(\frac{1}{(1 + [(Yield/100) \times (Days/Basis)])} \right)$$

This is a very commonly used and important formula, called the yield to discount formula. It enables you to discount amounts to their present values, and using yields, to convert quoted yields to discounts also.

Why is this formula constructed the way it is? An illustration will help.

Let us assume for a moment that we are working with a time fraction of one, typically produced by working with 360 days in a 360 day year for instance. Our rate of yield is 10%. Thus 100 will grow to 110 in a year. We have actually multiplied 100 by 1.10 and get 110. Thus if we know the end result is 110, how do we get back to the start? By reversing the procedure. Instead of multiplying, we divide, thus:

$$110/1.10 = 100$$

If you look at the formula above you will note that, in exactly the same way we are dividing by the appropriate proportion of the yield.

Returning to our problem:

We have an obligation to deliver a fixed amount of £1,500,000 to a client in 182 days. (i.e. we know the desired end result). If we buy sterling, how much do we need to invest TODAY at a money market yield of 8.125% p.a. to give us £1,500,000 in 182 days time?

Substituting

$$PV = 1,500,000 \left(\frac{1}{(1 + [8.125/100 \times 182/365])} \right)$$
$$= 1,500,000 \times 0.961064$$
$$= 1,441,595.63$$

This can be proven correct by calculating the simple interest on £1,441,595.63 as shown in earlier sections, and adding it on. You should attain precisely £1,500,000. As a general rule, it can be a useful check on some calculations, and this is typical, to work them backwards afterwards, to check your arithmetic.

The right hand side of the equation exclusive of the amount [0.961064] is sometimes called the "discount factor" relating to a yield of 8.125% p.a. yield for 182 days.

The keystrokes for the HP12C are as follows, but bear in mind that you will need to work out the decimal equivalent of the time fraction:

i.e. 182 days on a 365 day basis is $182/365 = 0.498630$

Problem

We have an obligation to deliver a fixed amount of £1,500,000 to a client in 182 days. If we buy sterling, how much do we need to invest TODAY at a money market yield of 8.125% p.a. to give us £1,500,000 in 182 days time?

Key	Display
182	
ENTER	
365	
÷	
n	
8.125	
i	
1,500,000	
FV	
PV = = = = >	− 1,441,595.63

Note that the cashflow sign on the final answer indicates that an amount of £1,441,595.63 must be invested i.e. negative cashflow at the start to achieve a positive cashflow at the end of £1,500,000.

The signing of cashflows is not perhaps essential at this elementary stage, but it is always a good habit to adopt so that in more advanced areas it is habitual when it is essential. When paying away a sum, precede it with a minus, when receiving a sum, leave it unsigned and therefore positive.

Once again, this sequence can be used *ad infinitum*, merely by substituting a different figure. Change the yield to 8.50%.

Key	Display
8.5	
i	
PV = = = = >	− 1,439,009.65

Our revised initial investment appears.

Change another parameter, but note that *you cannot solve for n* and cannot therefore calculate the number of days required to reach a target figure.

3.6.4 Accumulated value calculations using discounts

There are a few occasions when it is necessary to calculate the future value of a sum that has been discounted, using the discount rate as distinct from the yield rate. More important, the formula used is also employed to convert discount rates to true yields, the subject of a later section.

Problem

You have received a payment of $584,232.56 being the discounted proceeds of a 90-day bill. The discount rate was 7.375% p.a., what was the face value of the original bill (actual/360 basis)?

First of all, you cannot simply add on 7.375% of the discounted amount in simple interest, adjusted for 90 days. This is only possible if the rate was a true yield rate.

The formula that is used is the fourth main formula that we need and is derived from an earlier one.

$$PV = FV(1 - [Days/Basis \times Discount/100])$$

Here we don't want the Present Value but the Future Value. The formula is therefore manipulated into:

$$FV = PV \left(\frac{1}{(1 - [(Days/Basis) \times (Discount/100)])} \right)$$

We are now in a position to solve the original problem by substitution.

Revisiting our problem:

You have received a payment of $584,232.56 being the discounted proceeds of a 90-day bill. The discount rate was 7.375% p.a., what was the face value of the original bill (actual/360 basis)?

Substitute

$$FV = 584,232.56 \left(\frac{1}{(1 - [90/360 \times 7.375/100])} \right)$$
$$= 584,232.56 \times 1.018784$$
$$= \$595,206.68$$

Once again, this can easily be proved, using simple interest calculations (and the discount rate):

$595,206.68 - 7.375\%$ for 90 days $= 584,232.56$ precisely

The best procedure for the HP12C follows. NOTE THAT YOU CANNOT USE THE n, i, PV and FV KEYS in this case, because they will produce an answer based on a YIELD RATE not, as required in this case, based on the DISCOUNT RATE. This unfortunately means working the formula through the machine, but using it intelligently will cut some corners.

We will continue using the same problem.

Key	Display
1	
ENTER	
90	[or input DAYS]
ENTER	
7.375	[or input DISCOUNT RATE]
X	
36000	[or input BASIS]
÷	
—	
1/x	(reciprocal key)
584,232.56	[or input PV AMOUNT]
X = = = = >	$595,206.68

The RECIPROCAL KEY is used here. Note that this key will become increasingly useful in later sections because of the number of occasions a formula using "1 over XYZ" format is used.

3.6.5   True yield rate to true discount rate conversion

Introduction

In certain markets, as we have seen, rates are quoted as true discounts, Acceptances, Commercial Paper and US Treasury Bills for example. In other markets, Money Markets, US Treasury Bonds, UK Gilts and Eurobonds, rates quoted are true yields.

With this situation, the investor must be able to judge what the best return on any investment opportunity is likely to be, but can only do so on the basis of comparing like with like. What yield in investment "x" must I look for, to compare with the discount rate quoted in investment "y"?

Problem

What gives the best three-month return to the investor?

1. 90-day Eurocommerical Paper issued by a bank (discount rate 7.25)

48

2. 90-day Eurodollar Deposit at the same bank, (yielding 7.30% p.a.)

Fundamentally, we are not comparing like with like. In previous sections, we have demonstrated that a yield is always higher than its equivalent discount. Number 2 looks better on its face, but is it really?

Recapping for a moment:

Information:

Amount $100
Rate 10%
Period 1 year

Yield:

Borrow 100 Repay 110 = = = = > interest $10 (Return 10/100 = 10.00%)

Discount:

Borrow 90 Repay 100 = = = = > interest $10 (Return 10/90 = 11.11%)

For "return" now read true yield. What we have demonstrated is that a discount of 10% corresponds to a true yield of 11.11%. The yield is ALWAYS higher.

A formula that we have already seen will enable us to change a YIELD to a DISCOUNT, and will therefore allow us to compare the two investments on the same DISCOUNT basis.

The yield to discount formula

$$\text{DISCOUNT} = \text{YIELD}\left(\frac{1}{1 + [(\text{Yield}/100) \times (\text{Days}/\text{Basis})]}\right)$$

Returning to the original problem:

Problem

What gives the best three-month return to the investor?

1. 90-day Eurocommercial Paper (discount rate 7.25)
2. 90-day Eurodollar Bank Deposit (yielding 7.30% p.a.)

Convert the deposit yield to a discount for comparison purposes:

$$\text{DISCOUNT} = 7.30 \left(\frac{1}{1 + (7.30/100 \times 90/360)} \right)$$
$$= 7.30 \times 0.982077$$
$$= 7.1692\%$$

Conclusion

The Eurocommercial Paper at 7.25% for 90 days is worth more than the Eurodollar Bank Deposit at 7.1692% both on discount basis.

The formula used previously to calculate Present Value given a Future Value and a True Yield can thus be used to convert true yields to true discounts. Note the rule mentioned earlier still applies, when a yield rate is used in the formula the "plus" sign must be present in the bottom line.

HP12C Procedure – Yield to Discount conversion

Problem

What gives the best three month return to the investor?

1. 90-day Eurocommercial Paper (discount rate 7.25)
2. 90-day Eurodollar Bank Deposit (yielding 7.30% p.a.)

Key	Display
90	
ENTER	
360	
÷	
n	
7.30	

i

ENTER

FV

PV $= = = = >$ -7.1692

Note: The ENTER key acts as a break to avoid keying in the yield twice.

This procedure basically discounts the rate of yield, for the period at that rate of yield.

3.6.6 True discount rate to true yield rate conversion

Returning to the introduction in the previous section, the converse is true, in that there is the same need, but this time to compare returns on different investment media, by converting the discount rate to an equivalent yield. In practice, it is likely that this, the discount to yield conversion would be used more often, since the majority of investments are expressed as yields in the market place.

Since we will use a formula to do this which employs a given discount rate, bearing in mind the rule of signs again, the formula must employ a "$-$" sign.

The same example is used again, for comparison purposes:

What gives the best three-month return to the investor?

  1. 90-day Eurocommercial Paper (discount rate 7.25)
  2. 90-day Eurodollar Bank Deposit (yielding 7.30% p.a.)

This time, as is more usual in practice, convert the discount rate to a true yield, for comparison with that of the deposit.

The formula is called:

The discount to yield formula

$$\text{YIELD} = \text{DISCOUNT} \left(\frac{1}{(1 - [(\text{DISCOUNT}/100) \times (\text{Days}/\text{Basis})])} \right)$$

$$\text{YIELD} = 7.25 \frac{1}{(1 - [7.25/100 \times 90/360])}$$

$$= 7.25 \times 1.018460$$

$$= 7.3838\%$$

Conclusion

The Eurocommercial Paper at 7.3838% yields more than the Bank Deposit at 7.30%.

The formula used previously to calculate Future Value given Present Value and a True Discount Rate, can also be used to convert true discounts to true yields.

HP12C procedure – Discount to Yield conversion

Problem

What gives the best three-month return to the investor?

1. 90-day Eurocommercial Paper (discount rate 7.25)
2. 90-day Eurodollar Bank Deposit (yielding 7.30% p.a.)

Key	Display
1	
ENTER	
7.25	
ENTER	
90	
X	
36000	
÷	
—	
1/x	
7.25	
X = = = = >	7.3838

An alternative way of converting a discount to a yield using the HP12C, employs the n, i, PV and FV keys.

Key	Display
1	
FV	
90	
ENTER	
360	
÷	
n	
7.25 (the discount rate)	
ENTER	
100	
÷	
90	
x	
360	
÷	
1	
−	
PV	
i = = = = >	7.3838

This seems more complicated at first, but does allow you to change the parameters at will. What you are doing is calculating the yield from an amount after discount for 90 days at 7.25% p.a. and calculating what it yields to the original amount in 90 days. Some may find it more satisfactory with experience, because a formula does not need to be memorised.

3.7 Summary of formulae

At this point it will be useful to summarise the formulae so far:

1. Discounted amount from face value (given discount rate)

$$PV = FV \ (1 - [(D/100) \times (t/\text{Basis})])$$

where
        PV = Discounted amount
        FV = Value at maturity (face value)
        D = True discounted rate
        t = Number of days in interest period

Calculates Present Value from Future Value, given Quoted Discount.

2. Discounted amount from face value (given yield rate)

$$PV = FV \left(\frac{1}{(1 + [(Y/100) \times (t/\text{Basis})])} \right)$$

where
        PV = Discounted amount
        FV = Value at maturity (face value)
        Y = True yield rate
        t = Number of days in interest period

Otherwise known as the Yield to Discount formula.

Calculates Present Value from Future Value given Quoted Yield.

3. Accumulated value at maturity (given yield rate)

$$FV = PV \ (1 + [(Y/100) \times (t/\text{Basis})])$$

where
        FV = Accumulated value at maturity
        PV = Initial principal amount
        Y = True yield rate
        t = Number of days in interest period

Calculates Future Value from Present Value, given Quoted Yield.

4. Face value at maturity (given discount rate)

$$FV = PV \left(\frac{1}{(1 - [(D/100) \times (t/\text{Basis})])} \right)$$

where

FV = Face or accumulated value at maturity
PV = Discounted amount/initial principal
D = True discount rate
t = Number of days in interest period

Otherwise known as the Discount to Yield formula.

Used to convert true discounts to true yields.

Note

The word "maturity" means the end of a single interest period, which may or may not be the final maturity date of an instrument.

3.8   Certificate of Deposit calculations

Single interest periods

3.8.1   Introduction

In order to understand the rationale behind the mathematics of CD pricing, a little basic knowledge of the instrument will be helpful.

A single interest period Certificate of Deposit or "CD" is an instrument issued by a bank, licensed deposit taker or a building society, (but not a company) to fund itself mostly in the short term. The certificate will be for a specific amount deposited, quote a rate of interest and a maturity date, when principal and interest will be repaid to the investor who holds it.

The most important characteristic of the CD is its resale ability. A fixed bank deposit with which it can be compared does not have the benefit of a secondary market. This means that the investor with a liquidity problem is in a better position with a CD than with an "unbreakable" deposit.

Scenario

A corporate client with £1,000,000 to deposit not unnaturally seeks the finest rates, while wishing to avoid undue credit and liquidity risk. A three-month deposit period is envisaged, but the treasurer does not want to be completely locked in for the period, in case cash flow problems arise and the deposit needs to be liquidated at short notice.

A three-month fixed bank deposit gives a good yield, but there is practically no possibility of breaking this, should the need arise.

An alternative is to purchase a sterling CD. They also give a good return, but can be resold in the secondary market that exists for these instruments. Because of this negotiability, the comparative yields of CDs as against deposits are slightly lower.

In either case, whether deposit or CD, the investor accepts some element of interest rate risk, should the need to sell arise. Credit or counterparty risk is the same, assuming the bank issuing the CD is the same as the bank accepting a deposit.

3.8.2   The yield of a CD held to maturity

Most CDs repay principal together with interest at maturity. A few only, are discounted. (Discounted instruments are covered elsewhere.)

The value of a CD held to maturity is determined using the following formula, which we have already encountered:

$$FV = PV \left(1 + [(Yield/100) \times (Days/Basis)]\right)$$

Example

What will be the maturity value of a three-month (90-day) CD yielding 8.25% p.a. if the investor pays £1,000,000 for it at the time of issue?

$$FV = 1,000,000 \left[1 + (8.25/100 \times 90/365)\right]$$
$$= 1,000,000 \times 1.0203424658$$
$$= £1,020,342.46$$

HP12C procedure

Key	Display
1	(amount)
CHS	(negative cashflow for investing)
EEX	
6	(amount)
PV	
90	(days to maturity)
n	
8.25	(yield or coupon as it can be called in this case)
i	
f INT	
R↓	(these keystrokes calculate
x > <y	on a UKMM basis)
+ = = = = >	1,020,342.47

An alternative way and better in some respects is as follows:
(Warning: HP19 users must NOT use this sequence; it is not accurate)

Key	Display
1	
CHS	
EEX	
6	
PV	
8.25	
i	

90

ENTER

365

÷

n

FV = = = = >   £1,020,342.47

3.8.3   Pricing the CD in the secondary market

Having calculated what our CD will be worth at maturity, when it is repaid together with interest or coupon, we now need to examine what happens should our investor need to recover his money from the investment before it matures. This, after all, is one of the reasons CDs are used. They can be sold, or traded in a secondary market. The principle of pricing a CD in the secondary market rests on valuing it at current yields, not at the original CD yield at time of issue.

This means that our three-month CD at 8.25% will be worth proportionately less with two months to maturity, if two-month yields generally have risen above 8.25% p.a. If two-month yields are lower after a month, then 8.25% p.a. is worth correspondingly more.

The valuation is carried out by discounting total value at maturity, at the current yield.

A formula to carry this out will be a combination of the Accumulated Value of a Yield formula and the Yield to Discount formula.

Accumulated Value formula (given yield)

$$MV = IV (1 + [(g/100) \times (m/Basis)])$$

MV = Maturity value
IV = Initial or investment value
g = coupon
m = period of CD

This is the simple accumulated value formula with MV and IV substituted.

Multiply this by the discount factor obtained from:

The Yield to Discount formula

$$DF = \frac{1}{1 + [(i/100) \times (Dm/Basis)]}$$

where

DF = Discount factor
Dm = Days to maturity
i = Current yield

Return to the same example.

What will be the maturity value of a three-month (90-day) CD yielding 8.25% p.a. if the investor pays £1,000,000 for it at the time of issue?

Question

What will it be worth after 12 days, when yields have risen to 8.50% p.a.?

1. Calculate the maturity value as before.
2. Discount this at the current yield, (8.50) for the number of days left to maturity (90 − 12).

Substituting

$$1,000,000 \times (1 + [8.25/100 \times 90/365])$$

$$= £1,020,342.47$$

now discount this amount

$$1,020,342.47 \times \frac{1}{(1 + [8.50/100 \times (90 - 12)/365])}$$

$$= \frac{1.020.342.47}{1.018164}$$

$$= 1,002,139.23$$

HP12C procedure

The aim of the HP12C procedure is to escape the formulae and we can do just that. We will recap on calculating the maturity value we did earlier and go straight on to calculate the secondary market value.

Key	Display
1	
CHS	
EEX	
6	
PV	note the negative number, for investing cashflow
8.25	
i	the coupon on the CD
90	
ENTER	
365	
÷	90 days as a fraction of the 365-day year
n	
FV = = = = >	£1,020,342.47 (the maturity value we found earlier)

Now we will proceed to discount this back 78 days, to its present value today, at a rate of yield in the market now, of 8.50%. Do not disturb the calculator.

Key	Display
8.50	
i	inputs the current yield
78	
ENTER	
365	

$\div$	78 days as a fraction of the year
n	inputs reminder of CD period
PV	Present value of the CD is £1,002,139.23

Precisely the same answer we had from the formula, but much easier. We have taken the FV of the CD and discounted to its PV over 78 days at a rate of yield of 8.50%. In other words, a dealer who buys this off the investor at a price of £1,002,139.23, will get £1,020,342.47, in 78 days time, a yield of 8.50% p.a.

At this point, you will now be beginning to appreciate the ability to go backwards and forwards in time (and value) using the FV to PV and PV to FV sequence on the calculator, using "n" to reflect the time involved and "i" as the rate of yield. It is worth reiterating the comment made earlier that yield can be either coupon or capital growth or a combination of both. Present value and accumulated value calculations done in this way, will soon become second nature.

Back to our CD. The market price of the CD will be £1,002,139.23 after 12 days when comparative yields (that is yields on similar instruments, with similar maturities), have risen to 8.50. This procedure, however, allows indefinite changing of parameters in the calculations. For example, change the yield to 8.25%, which you will recall is the yield on the *original* CD:

Key	**Display**
8.25	
i	
PV = = = = >	£1,002,665.23

The CD would have been worth this latest amount if yields had remained unchanged. Note, however, that this number is lower than the CD value of £1,000,000 plus accrued interest for 12 days, which is £1,002,712.33. The reason for this, is that even though you are selling the security at the same yield as you bought it, you are receiving the 12 days' accrued interest, some 78 days earlier than would have been the case if you had held the CD to maturity. Thus, the 12 days' interest is discounted to its present value.

This is a little complicated so perhaps we should examine it a little more closely and a summary of some of the numbers we have already worked out, will be useful for clarification.

Information summary

CD value at the beginning   £1,000,000.00
CD value at the maturity   £1,020,342.47 (yields 8.25 after 90 days)

With days elapsed 12 and days to maturity 78 (90 – 12)
Yields remain 8.25, for 78-day instruments.

Accrued interest = 1,000,000 at 8.25% for 12 days is £2712.33
Value of principal sum at maturity = £1,000,000.00

Now, discount the accrued interest "FVs" back to its PVs at 8.25 for 78 days:

Key	Display
78	
ENTER	
365	
÷	
n	
8.25	
i	
2712.33	
FV	
PV = = = = >	2665.3397 (present value of accrued interest)

Add this to the principal at maturity of £1,000,000 and we have the price of the CD today. What if the selling yield rate is higher, say at 8.50%

p.a. that we used earlier, then the accrued interest and principal is discounted at 8.50%. The key to this is to be found in the next section. What is important is the price to the buyer in the secondary market. The price of £1,002,665.34 growing to the fixed maturity value of £1,020,342.47 will inevitably give a yield of 8.25 to the buyer. What if the buyer seeks a higher yield? The price must come lower and that means, if necessary that the principal sum itself may be discounted. If yields rise high enough in the secondary market after a very short time (we used 12 days remember) the investor can find that to sell, giving the quoted yield to the new buyer, can involve receiving a price of *less than face value* of £1,000,000.00.

A final example will demonstrate this:

90 CD for $1,000,000.00 with a coupon of 10% on a USMM basis (act/360), will yield a final value at maturity of $1,025,000.00.

If yields rise to 12% and the security is sold after 5 days, with 85 to maturity, it will be worth only $996,758.51.

Accrued interest after 5 days = $1,388.89 (PV of this at 12% is $1350.62). The CD is not worth $1,001,350.89 however, so the principal sum has been affected too.

3.8.4   Calculating effective yield to buyer and seller

There are two final calculations to make, the first of which will clarify some of our earlier work in the preceding section. As we discussed, the yield at which the CD sells in the secondary market is the key to its price. The price shown to the seller by the buyer must result in the buyer actually getting the yield quoted.

Effective yield to the new holder of the CD

In one of our earlier examples we used 8.50% as the selling yield in the secondary market. Let us return to that.

Recapping:

   Amount £1,000,000.00

Coupon 8.25
Maturity 90/365 days
Maturity value including coupon £1,020,342.47
Sold after 12 days (78/365 to maturity) at a new yield of 8.50
Price £1,002,139.23

We have established that the £1,002,139.23 is the discounted value of the sum at maturity which is guaranteed as £1,020,342.47. It follows therefore that if you buy a cash flow now, worth £1,020,342.47 in 78 days, for a price of £1,002,139.23, it grows at an annual rate of yield of 8.50% p.a.

In theory it is calculated as the annualised percentage difference between purchase price and maturity value.

There are two ways to calculate this using the HP12C. It is calculated as the annualised percentage difference between purchase price and maturity value (assuming it is so held).

Method One:

Key	Display
78/365	(on the assumption that you can now do the arithmetic of the time fraction)
n	
1,002,139.23	
CHS	
PV	(price you pay in secondary market)
1,020,342.47	
FV	(value received at maturity)
i = = = = >	8.50 (the yield to the buyer)

Method Two:

As an alternative, you can use the △% key and annualise the result yourself:

Key	Display
1,002,139.23	
ENTER	
1,020,342.47	
$\triangle\%$ = = = = >	1.82
78	
÷	
365	
x = = = = >	8.50%

Conclusion

An investment of £1,002,139.23 for 78 days yielding £18,203.24 simple interest, plus principal at maturity has a total yield of 8.50% p.a.

The only remaining calculation is to look at the final yield to the seller of the Certificate.

You should appreciate that the original holder of the CD having sold it, albeit early, has now received not only his principal amount of £1,000,000.00 but £2,139.23 in yield as well. He has however received the principal and accrued interest earlier than he would have done if he had waited until the maturity of the CD. Thus this interest should always be discounted to its present value, along with the principal.

Earlier we calculated the price of the CD, with an unchanged yield of 8.25% as £1,002,665.23 after 12 days. If you calculate the Accumulated Value of £1 million at 8.25% p.a. after 12 days, you get an answer of (a) £1,002,712.33 not (b) £1,002,665.23. The discrepancy arises because (b) represents principal, plus accrued interest discounted for 78 days to Present Value.

Thus the yield of a CD paying an 8.25% coupon, sold after 12 days on the same yield, actually yields 8.11% p.a. The question is why?

Returning to our original problem, we had the following information. The investor bought the CD for £1,000,000 with a coupon of 8.25%. It was resold after 12 days at a yield of 8.50% and this gave a price of £1,002,139.23. The calculator makes this computation relatively simple.

Key	Display
1,000,000	
CHS	
PV	
12	
ENTER	
365	
÷	
n	
1,002,139.23	
PV	
FV = = = = >	6.51%

The investor has suffered quite a penalty, by having to liquidate after only 12 days, after a 25 basis point rise in yields.

Before concluding the final section, let us look at the last sequence in PV and FV terms.

What did the original CD holder pay?	£1,000,000.00
What did he receive for his CD?	£1,002,139.23
How long was it held?	12 days

What is the annualised rate of growth over this period?

Key	Display
1,000,000.00	
ENTER	
1,002,139.23	
△% = = = = >	0.21% (flat rate)

365

x

12

$\div\ =\ =\ =\ =\ >$ 6.51%

In order to recover this interest loss, it would be necessary to reinvest the principal and interest in a 78-day security, yielding 8.50%, which is the same as holding the original investment to maturity. This demonstrates the effect of interest rate exposure, in what amounts to a short-term fixed interest security, as yields rise, so prices fall, a principle which we see in fixed rate bond markets. The example using the US dollar CD, in which we actually saw a capital loss, demonstrates that if yields change dramatically enough, the eventual yield to the original holder who is forced to sell, can even be negative.

3.9   US Treasury Bills

The calculation of discount rate and bond yield equivalent on six-month Treasury Bills

In an earlier part of this manual, we considered day-year calculations and later, discount to yield conversions (and vice versa). In this part, we review these principles and demonstrate their simultaneous use in combination.

There are often occasions when an investment decision has to be made on the basis of comparative returns. For example, in terms of yield, is a given US Treasury Bill a better investment than a given Treasury Bond? To do this you must always make sure you are comparing like with like.

Information

Treasury Bills
Usually quoted at a discount, they are non interest-bearing in that they are purchased at a discount below par and redeemed at par, the capital growth being treated as income. Initial maturities are three, six and twelve months. Day-year basis is Actual/360 (USMM).

Treasury Bonds
Quoted as a semi-annual yield (yield to maturity strictly speaking, but

the whole question of yield to maturity is covered in greater depth elsewhere. Initial maturities of 15 to 30 years. Day-year basis is Actual /Actual.

Note

At this stage, since we are still concerned with simple interest, we will make a direct comparison with a six-month US T-bill and a US T-bond paying a semi-annual coupon. The question of the frequency of coupon payment is a third factor which should be taken into account, but this necessity is eliminated by using a six-month T-bill at this stage. Frequency and effective rate calculations will be considered in the chapter on compound interest. If we were to compare three-month bills with bonds, then we should acknowledge that the frequency of coupon payment on them is twice that of the T-bond.

Here there are two principal differences between the two instruments:

(a) The yield convention (yield or discount quotation).
(b) Day-year convention.

These must both be taken account of for comparison purposes.

Problem

A six-month US Treasury Bill is quoted as follows:

Value date:	June 8th 1990
Price:	95.344 (actually 95 11/32)
Redemption value:	100.00
Redemption date:	December 8th 1990

What sort of equivalent yield would you be looking for in a US Treasury Bond?

Tasks: 1. Establish the exact number of days to maturity.
      2. Establish the annualised discount rate.
      3. Convert this to annualised yield.
      4. Convert to correct day-year basis.

1. Using the HP12C calendar function, making sure the date convention (M.DY or D.MY) is set correctly (see "Setting up the HP12C").

Key	Display
8.061990	
ENTER	
8.121990	
g△DYS = = = = >	183.000000

Maturity −183 calendar days

2. Annualised discount rate

$$100 - 95.344 = 4.656\% \text{ for 183 days}$$

$$4.6560 \times \frac{360}{183} = 9.16\% \text{ p.a.}$$

3. Convert to yield rate (using *discount to yield* formula)

Key	Display
9.16	
ENTER	
ENTER	
36000	
÷	
183	
X	
1	
−	
1/x	
X = = = = >	9.61% p.a.

The equivalent yield of a discount rate of 9.16% is 9.61% p.a. for 183 days.

An alternative way of calculating the discount to yield conversion, is given below. This method allows the changing of parameters, for "what if" exercises. It actually calculates the annual yield for a fraction of the year using the price of the bill.

Key	Display
−95.344	(invest in price of bill)
PV	
183	
ENTER	
360	
÷	
n	
100	
FV	
i = = = = >	9.61%

4. Convert the yield from a 183/360 basis to 183/365 basis

Note

The T-bill basis is a bigger time fraction than the T-bond basis. The T-bond yield sought must be quoted higher to achieve a comparable return.

Leave 9.61 in the calculator:

Key	Display
365	
X	
360	
÷ = = = = >	9.74%

Conclusion

A T-bond quoted at 9.74% p.a. yield will give the same yield as a 183-day T-bill priced at 95.344.

The method outlined above uses a set of logical procedures which have already been covered in earlier parts of the handbook, but which have been chained together in stages. There is a single formula which will be quicker for day-to-day use, but this does not clearly demonstrate the mathematical principles involved. The formula is as follows:

$$\frac{\text{Discount Rate}}{\text{Price}} \times \frac{365}{360} \times 100$$

substituting figures from the earlier example:

$$\frac{9.16}{95.344} \times \frac{365}{360} \times 100$$

$$= 9.61 \times \frac{365}{360}$$

$$= 9.74\%$$

This achieves the same result.

4 Compound interest calculations

4.1 Compound interest theory

The theory of compound interest as distinct from simple interest takes into account the fact that interest itself earns interest. An investment of $1 million in a fixed rate Eurodollar Bond paying a coupon (interest) of 7.00% per annum, will give a return of $70,000.00 every year, because by convention, Eurobonds pay interest once a year.

Compare this with an identical amount invested in a US Treasury Bond, which pays interest at the rate of 7.00% p.a., but with half of the annual coupon paid every six months (semi-annual or s.a.). Assuming that all coupons are reinvested at the same rate, this means that the amount invested for the second interest period increases by the amount of interest paid in the first period. The total earnings at the end of the year are therefore $1,071,225.00.

This can be demonstrated thus:

    $1 =$ Principal amount invested at the beginning
    $i =$ Interest earned each interest period

Total amount at the end of the first period	$(1 + i)$
Reinvest $(1 + i)$ at rate of i gives interest of	$i(1 + i)$
Total amount at the end of second period	$(1 + i) + i(1 + i)$

This can be simplified as follows:

$$(1 + i) + i(1 + i)$$
$$1 + i + i + i^2$$
$$(1 + i) \times (1 + i)$$
$$(1 + i)^2$$

72

A general question can therefore be written as follows:

$$Y = \frac{(1 + i)^n}{100}$$

where
    i = periodic simple yield
    n = number of periods
    1 = principal amount
    Y = compounding factor for calculating total of principal and
        interest

Problem

How much will $1 million be worth in three years, at a coupon rate of 8.00%, paid annually?

$$\text{Substituting } Y = \left(1 + \left(\frac{8}{100} \right) \right)^3$$

$$Y = 1.259712$$

Multiply the principal amount by the compounding factor:

$$1,000,000 \times 1.259712$$
$$= \$1,259,712$$

This can be proved in two ways, using repetitive simple interest calculations, adding the interest back each time, before calculating the next periodic return.

First the cash–money route:

$$1,000,000 + 80,000 + 86,400 + 93,312 = 1,259,712$$

Secondly using periodic yields (yield for each period, here each of one year):

$$1,000,000 \times (1.08 \times 1.08 \times 1.08) = 1,259,712$$

The latter route demonstrating the compounding principles quite clearly.

From this we can move easily to consider Accumulated and Present Values for multiple interest periods.

Note

It will be assumed from this section onwards, that your existing mathematical knowledge will enable you to manipulate index numbers confidently. A short set of guide-lines is however included here as a reminder.

4.1.1 Indices

1. When multiplying identical numbers with indices together, add the index numbers.

$$2^2 \times 2^3 = [(2 \times 2)(2 \times 2 \times 2)] = 2^5$$

2. Conversely when dividing, subtract the index numbers.
3. The root of a number can be written as the power of the reciprocal of the index number.

Square root of 49 = 7

i.e. $49^{1/2}$ or $49^{0.50} = 7$

Fifth root of 1.08 = 1.015511

i.e. $1.08^{1/5}$ or $1.08^{0.20} = 1.015511$

The HP12C is well designed for complex root calculations. For example in compound interest, effective rate and swap calculations, it is often necessary to work out calculations such as the 4th root or even the 52nd root of a number. The following key strokes will facilitate this.

Question

The rate of yield per annum, for a one-year deposit is 10%. What rate should a money dealer quote for a one-week deposit that is effectively the same as this?

To solve this we will need to know the 52nd root of 1.10:

Key	Display
1.10	
ENTER	
52	
$1/\times$	
$Yx = = = = >$	1.001835
1	
—	
5200	
$X = = = = >$	9.54% p.a.

What we have actually done here is calculate the on-screen rate for one week money which if maintained at the same level and all interest is reinvested at that rate, would amount to 10% p.a. equivalent. This is complicated and is something we will look at again later. For now, it is just a practical example of how index numbers are used in financial arithmetic.

Note that the 52nd root is obtained by keying in 52, calculating with one keystroke, its reciprocal, and using that figure as the power, with one further keystroke.

Negative indices are not normally required in interest calculations.

4.2   Yields and accumulated values

Earlier it was demonstrated that a simple yield works forward to give an accumulated or future value at future maturity date. The principle as might be expected, works for a compounded yield as well.

Problem

What will be the accumulated value of $1,000,000, at a coupon rate of 6%, paid semi-annually for five years?

Digressing from the problem for a moment, a formula similar to the Accumulated Value formula for single periods can be used, modified in accordance with the compound interest theory.

$$FV = PV (1 + (i/100))^n$$

Where "n" is the number of periods involved. Note this is the "n" on the HP12C and the i is the *periodic* rate of yield.

Note

In all practical cases, a true yield rate is the rate quoted in the formula. The problem of using a true discount rate could arise as in the simple interest calculations earlier. In practice it never does, so we will only need one formula for Accumulated Value and one in the next section for Present Value calculations.

Returning to the problem:

What will be the accumulated value of $1,000,000, at a coupon rate of 6%, paid *semi-annually* for five years? Note that the *periodic* rate is 3% per six months.

$$FV = PV(1 + (i/100))^n$$

Substituting

$$FV = 1,000,000 (1 + 3/100)^{10}$$

$$= 1,000,000 \times 1.34391638$$

$$= \$1,343,916.38$$

Note

1. The creation of the compounding factor 1.34391638.
2. There is an alternative way of writing the formula using the annual rate of yield. Either way, you must eventually work with the number of interest periods (coupons payable) and the actual periodic rate, or amount in flat % paid.

$$FV = 1,000,000 \ (1 + 6/200)^{10} = 1,343,916.38$$

A general formula for this would be written:

$$FV = 1,000,000 \ (1 + (i/n \times 100))^{n \times t}$$

where

> n = Number of compounding periods in a year
> i = Annualised yield rate
> t = Number of years to maturity

It is probably easier to think in terms of the periodic rate and the number of periods since this falls in line with the *modus operandi* of the HP12C.

HP12C Procedure

General note
Now we are moving on into compound interest and bond calculations, it will make things rather easier if we change the format for entering data into the HP12C. While the linear format has allowed you to follow the keystrokes, step by step, up to now, it does make certain more complex techniques a little difficult to follow. From this point on, therefore, a revised layout will be used and assumptions will be made that you know how to enter data.

The following example, which continues the explanation of the theory so far, is presented in two ways for comparison. The second format is what we will use from now on.

Example

What will be the accumulated value of an investment of $1,000,000, at a coupon rate of 7.00%, paid semi-annually for three years?

N.B. 1. This uses the n, i, PV and FV keys.
     2. Correct cash flow signing is important.

Format One (which will be discontinued)

Key	Display
1	
CHS	
EEX	
6	
PV	
3.5	
i	
6	
n	
FV = = = = >	$1,229,255.33

Format Two (much easier and quicker to read)

What will be the accumulated value of an investment of $1,000,000, at a coupon rate of 7.00%, paid semi-annually for three years?

Key	Display
PV	− 1,000,000
i	3.50
n	6
FV = = = = >	1,229,255.33

Note

1. The number of interest (or compounding periods) goes into "n".
2. The rate for the periods goes into "i".
3. In other words, the rates and periods must be entered as you would if you were using the theoretical formula.

Inputting 3 into "n" and 7.00 into "i". *will not work*, as it represents 7.00% paid annually for three years, not 3.50% paid every six months, for three years. This is a question of effective rates and will be explored later.

Note on the PMT key

So far, we have not used this key, but will do so quite soon. Briefly, in a bond for example, yield may be made up of coupon and appreciation in price. For example, you might see a five-year Eurobond, priced at 95% of its face value, paying a coupon of 10% per annum, and redeeming (being repaid by the borrower at maturity) at 100%. This investment will pay 10% per year coupon and will, over its life appreciate at an average rate of 1% per year. The symbol "i" is the periodic rate of yield (combination of coupon and capital growth), whereas the "PMT" symbol represents coupon.

As a rule, for semi-annual yields, when you halve the rate put into *PMT*, you double the number of years in *n* and the *i* resulting is half its p.a. value.

When calculating quarterly, the number of years in *n* is multiplied by 4, the coupon and yield will be a quarter of their per annum value.

For a monthly scheme, such as a mortgage, or a monthly swap, multiply years going into key "*n*" by 12, and *PMT* and *i* will be a twelfth of their p.a. values.

This information is provided at this stage only, to answer the question of what PMT is, which you are probably asking already. You may rest assured that much more use will be made of this key later, when the principles will become much clearer.

4.3   Discounts and present values

Discounts essentially work in reverse to yields in both simple and compound interest situations. There will be many occasions when we need to know what the Present Value is of a future sum of money or a future cashflow or maturing instrument or loan. The future maturity date may be years away, and there may be several coupon payments to consider as well, each having to be valued at today's "Present Value" or PV.

Almost invariably, this will be done by discounting the Future Value (FV) using the chosen yield rate, to its PV or price.

An investor places funds in a seven-year bond which pays no interest, but which is available at a price below its maturity value of $1,000,000.00 (below par). The investor is informed by his broker that the yield on the bond, which is all capital growth and no coupon, is 8% p.a. How much should the investor pay for it? (Use annual compounding.)

Once again, digressing from the problem briefly, the formula for assessing Present Value from a given yield is the *yield to discount* formula, the reverse of the formula used to calculate FV, compounded of course.

$$PV = FV \left(\left(\frac{1}{1 + (i/100)} \right)^n \right)$$

Substituting

$$PV = 1,000,000 \left(\left(\frac{1}{1 + 8/100} \right)^7 \right)$$

$$= 1,000,000 \times 0.583490395$$

$$= \$583,490.40$$

Conclusion

For a yield of 8% p.a. the investor should pay no more than $583,490.40 for the bond, and hold until redemption.

Points to note

The use of the *discount factor* of 0.583490395. This can be proved by cumulative simple interest calculations, by using the HP12C:

Key

583,490.40	Stage 1
ENTER	Stage 2
8	Stage 3

| % | Stage 4 |
| + | Stage 5 |

Repeat Stages 3, 4, and 5 seven times

| = = = = > | 1,000,000.00 Stage 6 |

HP12C procedure

This uses the same keys, but the solution lies with the key PV, rather than the Accumulated Value sequence which solves for FV. The variations of course, are infinite. In this way, we begin to use the machine as it is supposed to be used. The TV keys, (Time Value, n, i, PV, PMT, and FV) can be regarded as rather like an equation, with up to five variables, substitute for four and you solve for the fifth. In this case you can substitute for as few as three and solve for the fourth. The fifth being zero.

Restating the problem, an investor places funds in a seven-year bond which pays no interest, but is quoted at a price below its maturity value of $1,000,000.00 (below par). The investor is informed by his broker that the yield on the bond, which is all capital growth and no interest, is 8% p.a. How much should the investor pay for it? (Use annual compounding.)

Key	Display
FV	1,000,000
i	8
n	7
PV = = = = >	− 583,490.40

Note that the "i" key gives the yield, if we substitute a different price. Our investor can only buy the quality and maturity of the type of bond that he wants at a price of $590,478.32. What yield does this represent?

Key	Display
PV	− 590,478.32
i = = = = >	7.8165

Note our use of the correct cashflow signs. It is not essential always to have them the right way round. As we shall see, it depends on whether you are looking at the problem from an investor's point of view, or an issuer's (the borrower). The important thing is to be consistent within a calculation, i.e. an investor always *pays* for bonds (negative cashflow), but *receives* income and redemption value (positive cashflow). Mixing investor and borrower will either produce an error message (5) or a strange result.

"What if" exercises can be done from this point, substituting the numbers you have to hand.

This substitution can be made indefinitely, but does not solve for the period ("n" key).

Further notes on the "n" key

It is important to note that you can only solve fractions of a year, for investment/borrowing periods of less than one year. For example, 180 days over 360 can be entered as $180/360 = 0.500$ quite safely, as one would with a loan type of instrument. However, with a bond, five years and 180 days *cannot* be entered as 5.500. This will produce a result which might look about right, but is not, so beware.

The reason for this is that in simple interest used in loans, we use $180/360$ format, so does the HP12C, but it uses this all the time, even for compound interest. The correct method for compound interest in bonds is to use a fractional index number, raising a sum to the power of 5.500 for example. In its simplest form it can be demonstrated as follows.

$100 at 10% p.a. for six months will grow to:

$$100 \times (1 + (10/100 \times 180/360) = \$105.00 \text{ (correct)}$$

an alternative way, using compound arithmetic would look like:

$$100 \times (1.10^{.50}) = 104.88 \text{ (incorrect for less than one year)}$$

Note for users who intend to move on to an HP19B at a later date
Be careful once again when using the finance function (TVM) on the

82

HP19B, because it is different yet again from the above procedures.

In short, you can use the HP12C "n" key for interest periods where the time fraction is less than 1 (e.g. 145 days/360). But with something like 3 years 180 days/360, which is greater than unity, this will not be accurate. With the HP19B, the reverse is true, you can use the TVM sequence, as it is called, for time fractions greater than unity, such as four half-year compound calculations, but not for periods of less than one year.

In both calculators, using fractions in the "n" key based on act/360, where a result like 362/360 is produced, the result will be unsafe in *both* HP12C and HP19B.

$100 at 10% p.a. for 6 months will grow to:

$$100 \times (1 + (10/100 \times 180/360) = \$105.00 \text{ (correct)}$$

HP12C uses this method.

An alternative way, using compound interest arithmetic would look like:

$$100 \times (1.10^{.50}) = 104.88 \text{ (incorrect for less than one year)}$$

HP19B uses this method.

4.4 Simple and effective rates

It is worthwhile at this point to reiterate the principle that a yield can be a matter of what periodic coupon or interest rate an investment pays (income), or what appreciation or depreciation (positive or negative capital growth) takes place from one point in the life of the investment to another, or for that matter a combination of both income and capital growth. Capital growth can be positive or negative of course.

Having covered compounded accumulated values, it is now necessary to distinguish between simple or nominal yield and effective yield.

Consider

Investment (A) is quoted as paying a rate of interest of 7.05% per annum. (Interest is paid once a year.)

Investment (B) is quoted as paying a rate of interest of 7.00% per annum. (Interest is paid in two equal six-monthly payments.)

The investor looking at the two alternatives, unaware of the frequency or significance of the timing of the coupon payments, would logically choose the investment that gives him the extra 5 basis points, (A).

He would be wrong. But why?

The reason is, that only the simple or nominal yield (for example what would appear on a data screen such as those produced by Reuters and Telerate in practice), is better in (A) than in (B). If the effective yield is calculated, this shows a different picture altogether. Effective yield takes into account the frequency of coupon payment and the fact that earlier coupon payments can be invested. In the example above, the investor in (B) will have the use of a 3.50% interest payment for six months, to reinvest. It is normally assumed that this will therefore be compounded at the coupon rate.

With this in mind, the true rate, or Effective Rate of Yield is 7.05% for (A) and 7.1225% for (B).

Terminology

Compound interest rates, or yields, can be referred to in two ways, simple and compound. In practice simple yields are referred to as "nominal" yields and compounded yields as "effective" yields. In practice, most yields in the market place are nominal yields. Their true value (effective rate) will be different if the coupon is payable more frequently than yearly.

For example, take the sterling time deposits, quoted by a London money broker on a data screen. These, without exception, are nominal rates. The six-month bid/offer is a semi-annual nominal rate; the one year, an annual nominal rate. In other words, the rate quoted to the market, whether in Time Deposit, Swap, or Bond, is the nominal rate. To compare one with another – a semi-annual yield with an annual yield – we will need to examine effective yields and this will ultimately enable us to make adjustments to one or other so that both are quoted nominally, on the same basis. This basis or *convention* is something we have already encountered in our examination of day-year adjustments. The question of frequency is the last of these conventions we need to look at.

How are effective yields calculated?

4.4.1   Simple/effective yield conversion

Effective yield from simple yield

The arithmetic is reasonably simple, if you remember basic compound interest principles. Remember also that what we are trying to do at this stage is to calculate what return we are really getting.

A depositor, investing $1.00 at 10% for one year, receives interest half yearly of $0.05. At the end of six months the accumulated value is $1.05. If this is all reinvested, we have: 1.05 × 1.05, or 1.1025. You can read off the effective rate of return as 10.25% p.a. from these numbers, by removing the leading digit "1" and moving the decimal point two places to the right. All we need to do is devise a formula to summarise these workings.

Refer back to the fully compounded Accumulated Value formula:

$$AV = PV \left([1 + (i/100)]^n \right)$$

where n = number of periods in the year
           i = the *periodic* simple, nominal rate

Substituting

$$AV = 1 \times \left([1 + 5/100]^2 \right)$$

$$= 1.1025$$

We can extract the 10.25% from this quite simply.

The full formula is thus:

$$EY = [([1 + (Yield/(n \times 100))]^n) - 1] \times 100$$

where

      n = the number of periods in the year and yield is the per annum nominal yield from the screen.

Note that the effective yield is always higher when the coupon frequency is increased.

We can now return to our original problem, to demonstrate the HP12C method.

Investment (A) is quoted as paying a rate of interest of 7.05% per annum. (Interest is paid once a year.)

Investment (B) is quoted as paying a rate of interest of 7.00% per annum. (Interest is paid in two equal six-monthly payments.)

Which is better? (Hint: calculate what both are really worth, "A" being 7.05% p.a.)

The HP12C procedure is straightforward, short cuts can be taken, with a little mental arithmetic, like inputting the periodic rate plus 1 straight-away (point x), and reading off the answer (at point y) without fully completing the procedure:

Key	**Display**
7	
ENTER	
200	
÷	
1	
+ = = = = >	1.0350 (x)

2

Y^x = = = = >   1.071225 (y)

1

—

100

X = = = = >   7.1225

For an effective annual from semi-annual rate, as here, input 1.0350, square it and read off the answer mentally moving the decimal point two places to the right after taking off the 1.

An alternative way, using the n, i, PV and FV (TVM) keys will also work, but requires a little interim arithmetic, such as working out the periodic rate and the number of periods per year, which should not tax one too much:

Key		Display
n	2	(2 for semi-annual, 4 for quarterly etc.)
i	3.50	(7/2 semi-annual, or 7/4 for quarterly etc.)
PV	1	(principal)
FV	= = = = >	1.071225

Then read off 7.1225 by dropping the leading one and moving the decimal point two places to the right as set out earlier.

Important note

This formula is also used to adjust semi-annual rates to annual equivalent.

Simple or nominal yield from effective yield

The reverse is less comfortable but straightforward. Where you squared, take the square root, to the power of four, take the fourth root etc., etc. This is why we covered such superficially esoteric calculations as the 52nd root, when we covered the arithmetic of indices.

Formula for nominal yield, given effective yield.

$$\left(\left[\sqrt[n]{\left(1 + \left(\frac{\text{Effective yield}}{100} \right) \right)} \right] - 1 \right) \times n \times 100$$

n = number of periods per year

It should be noted, that for practical purposes, the need to calculate nominal rate, given effective rate is probably fairly unusual. This does not however invalidate the procedure because, as we shall see, this sequence is very important in other ways.

Problem

What will be the nominal rate of interest to a borrower in a full year, if he is quoted an effective rate of 9.9375% charged quarterly, on £1,000,000? Note that for ordinary arithmetic, we revert to the old pattern of linear keystroke procedure.

Key	Display
9.9375	
ENTER	
100	
÷	
1	
+	
4	
1/x	(this sequence obviates the need for the use of a fourth root key)
Y^x	(by raising the number to the power of a quarter)
1	
−	
400	
x = = = = >	9.5873%

88

We can conclude from this that the nominal rate payable would be 9.5873% p.a.

Important note

This formula is also used to adjust an annual rate into a semi-annual equivalent.

Once again, for practical purposes, the use of the n, i, PV and FV keys gives a more satisfactory approach, because of the ability to change the parameters without the need to recalculate the result completely from the beginning. This time the known quantity is the effective rate, which goes into FV and we solve for "i".

Problem

What amount of interest will a borrower pay in a full year, if he is quoted an effective rate of 9.9375% charged quarterly, on £1,000,000?

Key	Display
n	4
FV	1.099375
PV	−1.00 (note that either FV or PV must be negative)
i = = = = >	2.3968
4x = = = = >	9.5873

Conclusion

The true cost will be higher. Nominal interest paid will be 9.5873% p.a. payable quarterly.

Summary of the two procedures involving the n, i, PV and FV keys

The number of compounding periods in the year always goes into "n". The figure 1 always goes into PV.

If solving for FV (the effective rate given the nominal or "screen" rate)

The periodic rate must go into "i" i.e., the nominal rate divided by "n". Solving for FV gives you 1 plus the decimalised effective rate, so strip out the leading figure 1 and move the decimal point two places to the right at all times.

If solving for i (the nominal rate given the effective rate)

The figure 1 plus the decimalised annualised <u>effective rate</u> goes into FV. Solving for "i" gives you the periodic rate of yield, which should be multiplied by the figure in "n".

4.5 Effect of compounding

To be aware of the effect of compounding on any quoted nominal rate is as essential as being aware of the effect of ignoring day-year calculations. It is a fundamental principle of interest rate exposure management. For example a corporate treasurer who ignores such an effect, and who is faced with the need to borrow money for a one year period, may have the option of borrowing for a year at 10% p.a. or for six months at 10% and a further six months at 9.80%. The latter route looks cheaper at first, but would in fact cost 15 basis points more over the year. The reason: compounding.

Another view. A traditional technique for making extra profit in lending money is mismatching. This can be done by lending for one period, say six months, and funding the operation by borrowing off the market for three months, on the assumption (a) that the shape of the yield curve is positive (upward sloping) and (b) that the three-month rate will stay constant or fall. Liquidity considerations would, of course, be important too.

For example: using the procedures outlined earlier, would it be cheaper for a corporate with a money market dealing facility, to fund itself for one year for a fixed amount on a weekly roll-over basis, or borrow the same amount for a full year?

Given: a positive yield curve.

Rates: 1 week   8.10–8.00
             1 year   8.40–8.30

Effective: 1 year = 8.40
1 week = ?
[answer: 8.43%]

This is calculated using techniques established earlier:

Key	Display
i	8.10/52 (periodic *weekly* rate)
n	52 (periods in the year)
PV	1
FV = = = = >	1.0843

We can read off the answer from this: 8.43% p.a. effective yield.

In this case, it is clear that the decision to roll over borrowing more frequently should include consideration of the effects of compounding, as well as the view of future interest rates.

Consider the effect of compounding daily for a full year, compared with monthly and six-monthly. A simple rate of 10.00% compounded becomes:

10.5156% daily

10.5065% weekly

10.4713% monthly

10.2500% semi-annually

10.0000% annually

The effect is a significant difference in the various yields. To put this in perspective, with swap spreads of some 5 basis points (0.05%), a mistake involving semi-annual/annual adjustment can make a difference of five times the spread.

Since this manual is intended as a practical guide, it is as well to note that daily compounding is a somewhat theoretical concept. In practice, interest is not payable on a non-working day, such as a Sunday or perhaps a Saturday, so to compound seven times each week would not be normal.

In this chapter, we made reference to a yield curve. In a later chapter, we will consider the structure of yield curves. The mathematical structure of money market yield curves also involves the compounding effect.

4.6   Conversions and comparisons

The final section dealing with the question of effective yields returns to the comparisons that must be made between different instruments for judgmental reasons, before investments are made.

It has already been demonstrated that adjustments must be made in respect of day-year basis and discount quotations compared to yield quotations to assess what is the "real" rate of return on an instrument. The question of interest payment (or coupon) frequency was mentioned in passing at the time, but eliminated by matching the two instruments. The ultimate in comparisons uses three adjustments. For example, to compare a 91-day US Treasury Bill (Quarterly, ACT/360, discount basis), directly with US Treasury Bond (semi-annual, ACT/ACT, yield basis) requires all three.

Preliminary note on gross redemption yield

Other considerations must be taken into account too. These are matters of market conventions and investor perception. When considering these questions you must consider the yield concept as embodying Gross Redemption Yield (GRY), which will include income and principal. Up to now we have tended to consider one or the other. The whole subject of yield to redemption is covered in detail in the next chapter, but from here onwards, when we speak of yield, we mean the total return.

Market conventions

Eurobonds have certain characteristics clearly defined by the AIBD used in the calculation of redemption yield. It will be as well to bear these in mind.

> "The standard method of calculating maturity yields shall be based on the definition of annual compounding, i.e. a bond with a 7% coupon, paying annually priced at 100%, yields 7% per annum and the same bond having interest semi-annually yields more."

US Treasury Bonds pay a semi-annual coupon.

A US investor seeking to invest in a Fixed Rate US dollar Bond is faced with the immediate choice of a US Government Bond, such as a T-bond, or a Eurodollar bond. These two markets have different conventions and the investor's perception of 8% in a US Treasury Bond would be different for a Eurobond.

4.7 Capitalisation of unpaid interest

A US investor in Eurobonds regards a given yield to maturity as less than a European investor.

The US investor normally expects a semi-annual coupon, the European investor, annual.

Therefore, a 10% coupon investment to the European does not have the same yield expectation to the US investor.

This can be demonstrated as follows.

Both investing in a 10% Eurodollar Bond:

Expectations

European:

Invests	100.00
Receives accrued interest expected	10.00
Total return	110.00

US:

Invests	100.00
Accrued interest expected	5.00
Total expected	105.00
Reinvested	105.00
Accrued interest expected	5.25
Total expected return	110.25

Conclusion

1. Despite their differing expectations both actually receive 110.00 by investing in a Eurobond.
2. The US investor must therefore seek out an extra 0.25 yield to attain the 10% yield that he is used to.

4.8 Capitalisation of unearned interest

The reverse of this is that the European investor in US securities may accept a lower yield than he would do otherwise.

In other words, the US investor must capitalise interest he sees as earned but unpaid in a Euro-security, whereas the European investor is in the situation of being able to capitalise interest paid but unearned, in terms of his normal expectations.

1. US investor – how to achieve that extra yield?
2. European investor – how the better US return may be used?

These expectations discussed above manifest themselves in the fact that bonds trade at, above or below par. Par is 100% of face value at redemption (repayment by the issuer or borrower). Most bonds (but not all) repay 100% of principal at maturity. These questions, again, are part of the wider subject of GRY, covered in the next section.

1. If a Eurobond pays a coupon of 10%, like it or not, then there is nothing the US investor can do about it. He cannot seek another with a 10.25% coupon to compensate. What he does is to find the extra yield by paying less than par for the bond. Capital growth plus income will make up 10.25% Gross Redemption Yield.

2. The European investor, being able to reinvest the semi-annual coupon of the T-bond which was not part of his normal expectation and push up his overall yield, can alternatively buy his security at a price above par, still maintaining his original yield expectation.

The conversion of US securities to Euro-securities and vice versa uses formulae and procedures already encountered.

These are repeated below.

US Treasury Bond to Eurobond equivalent conversion, i.e. quoting a semi-annual rate of yield on an annual basis. The less frequent coupon requires higher return to compensate:

$$E = ([1 + ((US/2) \times 100)^2] - 1 \times 100)$$

$$E = \text{Euro equivalent yield required}$$
$$US = \text{US T-bond yield}$$

Eurobond equivalent to US Treasury Bond conversion, i.e. quoting an annual rate of yield on a semi-annual basis. More frequent coupon will allow a lower rate of yield.

$$US = \left[\left(\sqrt{\left(1 + \left(\frac{E}{100}\right)\right)} \right) - 1 \right] \times 200$$

The HP12C procedures for changing US to Euro basis and vice versa are straightforward.

Annual coupon with annual compounding equivalent of semi-annual coupon with annual compounding

(US Treasury Bond on Eurobond basis)

Coupon of 8.00, what yield will US expectations require?

Key	or	**Key**	
8		n	2
ENTER		PV	−1
200		i	4
÷		FV	= = = = > 1.0816
1			
+		Read off as 8.16% p.a.	

2

Y^x

1

—

100

X = = = = >   8.16% p.a.

Semi-annual coupon with annual compounding equivalent of annual coupon with annual compounding

(Eurobond on US Treasury Bond basis)

Coupon of 8.16, what yield can European expectations accept?

Key	Display
8.16	
ENTER	
100	
÷	
1	
+	
g $\sqrt{x}$ = = = = >	1.04 (or read off and multiply by 200)
1	
—	
200	
X = = = = >	8.00

or

Key	
n	2
PV	−1

$$\begin{array}{lll} \text{FV} & & 1.0816 \\ \text{i} & ==== > & 4.00\% \text{ s.a. (which is doubled for the} \\ & & \text{annualised figure)} \end{array}$$

4.9 The term structure of interest rates – yield curves

Introduction

The term structure of interest rates, that is the mathematical relationship between the level of reward required (interest) for investing money and the length of time (maturity) that the investor is prepared to invest, is quite exact.

It takes into account the investor's views on the future direction and level of interest rates and is then arbitrage driven.

Let us take a simple example, assuming that one year deposit rates are at 10% p.a. and, I believe, likely to remain so. I have the ability to place $100 on deposit for two years. I have a number of choices, but will restrict it to two. Either I invest for one year and then roll over for another year at the one-year rate, in one year's time, or I invest for two years at the two-year rate today. In a perfect market, there should be no difference between the two.

The conclusion we will be able to draw from this is that the two-year rate today is governed through arbitrage, by the one-year rate today coupled with the forecast one-year rate, in a year's time. It is this which in turn governs the shape of so-called yield curves.

It should be noted that although yield curves are important to the manager of interest rate exposure, this chapter is not intended to set out in detail how such exposures should be managed.

Yield curves

A yield curve is a graphic representation of the levels of return for a range of maturities in a given instrument, at a specific time.

They are created by plotting yields in a single instrument on the vertical axis, against maturity on the horizontal axis. Although instruments should never be mixed in a single curve, it is quite common to overlay one yield curve with another, so that a comparison may be drawn at a glance, or even to plot the difference between two yield curves as a third, for analytical purposes.

For example, a fairly common comparison made by issuers of Commercial Paper is the relationship between an index of Commercial Paper rates and Libor (London Interbank Offered Rate).

General uses

The uses of yield curves mainly arise out of trying to forecast future trends and levels in interest rates as part of "interest rate exposure management" systems. In trying to do this one should be particularly careful about yield curve interpretation. Yield curves should never be looked at in static isolation, they are a dynamic representation of past activity in a given instrument, sometimes in anticipation of future events. As such they may be used as a forecasting medium and an analysis tool for a particular market sector.

In addition there are many reasons why a yield curve assumes a particular shape. It is not so much the static instantaneous shape you should be looking at, but the trend of the change in shape. Is it steepening? Is it flattening? More positive? More negative? Etc. In other words a "moving picture" gives you more information than a "still".

4.9.1 The shapes

Yield curves can be:

> *Positive* sometimes called normal (sloping up)
>
> *Negative* or inverted (sloping down)
>
> *Flat* (no slope)
>
> *Humped* (higher rates in the middle maturities)

These shapes are derived from a variety of activities in each of the respective markets. A number of theories exist which also purport to account for them and these are worth looking at. They should not be taken as gospel when forecasting, because technical factors often exist which cloud or even contradict theoretical conclusions.

Yield curve shapes produce certain effects in pricing hedging instruments that start on a future date, notably Forward Rate Agreements (FRAs) and Forward Start Swaps, and an appreciation of this is also useful. This will be covered in the chapter on forward–forward calculations.

Additionally, it will be useful to clarify some of the jargon associated with yield curves, which can seem a little curious.

When a yield curve is said to be *steepening*, it means that the far end is rising or the near end is falling or both. Curiously, even when a negative yield curve appears to be getting less steep, because yields in far maturities are rising, it is still said to be steepening. In other words, a steepening yield curve is swinging in an anti-clockwise direction.

When a curve is said to be *flattening*, it means that the far end is falling or the near end rising or both. Once again, with a negative yield curve, a curve that is technically flattening appears to grow more negative. In other words, a flattening yield curve is swinging in a clockwise direction.

When a curve moves upwards or downwards uniformly along its length, it is said to have developed a *parallel shift*.

At this point, we can now begin to look at the factors and influences that govern the shape of the yield curve.

Expectations theory

An upward sloping yield curve, particularly one that is steepening, may be interpreted as an indication that yields are expected to rise. Time horizon is difficult to determine, but the trend is upwards. The upward sloping yield curve is produced when borrowers, seeking to put off increased interest rate costs, borrow in the longer maturities. The investor, not wishing to be locked-in on a rising market, invests in shorter dated instruments (the near end of the yield curve), and reinvests later at a higher rate. The resulting increase in liquidity at the near end (lower rates) and shortage of liquidity at the long end (higher rates) produces a positive or anti-clockwise swing in the curve.

A negative yield curve may mean a future interest rate fall, and therefore potential borrowers and investors position themselves in the market accordingly, the reverse of the strategy above. Borrowers move to shorter maturities so that funding can be rolled over as soon as possible after a rate cut and investors seek to lock-in the existing higher rates for as long as possible, before they too become subject to lower yields.

A flat to negative sterling yield curve sometimes can be regarded as merely a transitional phase, between a negative curve becoming positive, or vice versa. Recent history would lead one to believe that the indication is one of uncertainty, when some think interest rates will fall in the not too distant future, but others are less certain.

Liquidity preference theory

This theory revolves around the liquidity preference of investors, which results in them calling for higher yields for locking up their money longer. You want a better rate on a five-year deposit than a one-year deposit. Additionally there are risks other than liquidity risk, which must be compensated for in longer investment periods. Inflation, credit risk and the effect of compounding also mean that to lock in for a longer period requires a better return. Thus a so-called "normal yield curve" takes these factors into account more than future perceptions of interest rate levels.

Supply and demand

Pure supply and demand also have a role to play in shaping the yield curve. For example, at the year end it is common for short-term interest rates to rise as this is the tax paying season when not only do companies borrow to meet their obligations but the cash paid to the Exchequer is removed from the system. The effect of this is often to invert the money market yield curve as short-term interest rates are forced up.

The Bank of England can of course control interest rates by making good any market shortage by, for instance, buying bills, or even taking more out of the market, by selling Treasury Bills at higher yields. Thus monetary policy itself has an effect on the shape of the curve.

4.9.2 Mathematical derivation from market rates

We can be rather more specific about what the shape of a yield curve implies. We can actually calculate what varying maturities should pay from expectations in the market place. In reverse, we can assess arithmetically what say, a one-year rate will be in one year's time from where two-year rates are on the yield curve.

To pick an example where perhaps one-year money is paying 13% and in a year's time it is predicted that one-year money will be paying 14%. Using these figures we can calculate what two-year money must pay today.

$$1.13 \times 1.14 = 1.2882$$

The total return on the investment over two years must be 28.82%. The square root of this is 1.134989, giving us a two-year rate of 13.4989% p.a. for two-year money.

In summary, the spot 12-month rate is 13.00% p.a. and the 12-month rate in a year's time is predicted at 14% p.a.

The spot rate for two years to achieve the same return will have to be 13.4989% p.a. (i.e. 13.4989% p.a. compounded over two years), produces the same return as 13% in year one and 14% in year two.

4.9.3 Implied future rates

To derive a numerical forecast from a yield curve, the reverse of the procedure outlined above can be used. That is to say an implied one-year rate in one year's time can be derived from the spot one-year and spot two-year, by simple algebra.

Note: Take two-year rate and compound it: $1.1350 \times 1.1350 = 1.2882$
Divide this figure by one-year rate of 1.13 gives 1.14
One-year rate implied in one year's time is 14%.

This will also work for yield curves, within the year, such as those encountered in money markets. Let us look at a two-month period, during which we either borrow for one month and roll over the loan for a second month, or we borrow for two months. In this case there is a slight difference to the principle we looked at earlier because if we borrow for a month and roll over, we compound at the flat monthly rate (annual/12). If, however, we borrow for two months, we do not compound at all because we only pay interest at the end of the two-month period, not monthly. The principles, nevertheless, hold good.

Sterling Libor rates might be quoted as follows, the yield curve being sharply negative:

    1 month 12.00%
    2 month 11.50%

What would we expect one-month money to trade at, in one month's time, from these numbers?

| One-month money costs | 1.0000% per month (compounded monthly) |
| Two-month money costs | 1.9167% per two months (not compounded at all) |

What is the effective cost of borrowing for <u>two months</u> at the one-month rate of 1% per month?

$$1.01 \times 1.01 = 1.0201$$

As we have done earlier, remove the leading digit 1 and move the decimal place two to the right, and we have 2.01%. Compare this with the actual cost of 1.9167% for two-month money.

For the final steps, we divide 1.019167 by 1.01, we get 1.009076, remove the "1" and move the decimal point, we have 0.9076. Multiply by 12 to annualise, gives 10.89% p.a.

Conclusion

If one-month money, in one month's time is 10.89% then lenders will be indifferent to lending for one month at 12% and one month at 10.89% or for two months at 11.50%. Thus we can say that the implied one-month rate in one month's time is 10.89% p.a.

4.9.4   The effect of compounding

An additional factor which governs the shape of a yield curve is the compounding effect, for periods of less than one year.

For example, given a simple rate of 10.00% per annum, for one-year money, the effective rate is 10.00%. A simple rate of 10.00% p.a. for six-month money, gives an effective rate of 10.25% per annum. Thus simple yields for one-year money must show a return of 10.25% to equate with a simple yield of 10.00% for six-month money. All other things being equal, this produces a positive, so-called normal, yield curve.

4.9.5   Additional types encountered

Par yield curve
This curve plots the coupons of bonds trading at par along the curve. Thus it is a plot of the coupons of these bonds.

Spot yield curve
All rates plotted are for maturities which start immediately.

Forward yield curve
Rates plotted for maturities starting on a certain forward date. These are technically forward–forward rates, for example 1s/2s, 1s/3s, 1s/4s etc., are one-month, two-month and three-month periods beginning in one month's time. A series of FRA prices represent such a curve.

4.9.6   The zero coupon yield curve

This plots the yields of instruments paying no coupon but where yield is made up of capital growth from a discount price. It can be calculated from the spot par yield curve (a curve which represents coupon or interest on investments which start immediately) and used to price a relatively risk-free series of cash flows for instruments such as Swaps. This is an important structure and we can explore its arithmetic in a little more depth.

First, a word or two about zero coupon structures. A zero coupon structure as one might imagine, pays no coupon at all, but sells at a deep discount. Returning to our theory of compound interest, a bond trading redeemable (repayable) at $100 in five years yielding 10% will currently be worth:

$$100/(1 + (10/100)^5)$$

$$= \$62.09$$

For reasons which we will cover later, if you buy this bond and hold it to maturity, credit risk aside, you are guaranteed $100 after five years, no matter what happens to bond yields in the interim. With a coupon bond, you are not, because coupons have to be reinvested at the same rate of yield, to maintain the yield of the bond at purchase. This may or may not be possible.

A zero coupon bond, thus represents an interest-rate-risk-free cashflow, provided it is not disturbed in any way prior to redemption. Zero coupon yield curves are therefore important in the Swap market, for example, because they too represent a relatively risk-free structure, a swap having cashflows much like a bond in some respects.

Let us assume the following spot par yield curve:

Year 1   7%
Year 2   8%
Year 3   9%
Year 4   10%

How do we construct a zero coupon yield curve from this, with numbers for year 1 through to year 4?

First of all, always assume a *PV of 1.00* for all future cash flows.

Thus for year 1, yielding 7% in the spot par yield curve, we have 1.00 now and we will have 1.07 in a year's time. This is a one-year zero coupon structure and so the number for one-year maturity on a zero coupon yield curve will be 7%.

What about the number for a two-year maturity zero coupon?

The cashflows for a two-year instrument (yielding 8% on the spot par yield curve), are as follows; this is worth 1.00 now, gives a cashflow of 0.08 in a year and 1.08 in two years. Next, discount the 0.08 in year one, at the one-year zero coupon rate of 7% p.a.

Key	Display
n	1.00
i	7
FV	0.08
PV ??? = = = = >	0.0748

So, the PV of the 8% coupon in a year is worth 0.0748. This means we have $(1.00 - 0.748 = 0.9252)$ remaining as the PV of the remaining cash flow in the two-year structure. The only other cashflow to come is 1.08 in two years, so at what rate does 1.08 have a PV of 0.9252? Work it out.

Key	Display
n	2.00
PV	-0.9252
FV	1.08
i	
??? = = = = >	8.04

From this we can say that if the one-year maturity on the zero coupon curve is 7%, then the two-year is 8.04%.

For year three, cashflows under the spot par yield curve (yield 9.00%) are:

Now	1 year	2 years	3 years
1.00	$0.09^{(1)}$	$0.09^{(2)}$	$1.09^{(3)}$

Using the zero coupon curve, discount the cashflows to their PV:

Key	Display
n	1.00
i	7 (one-year zero coupon rate)
FV	0.09
PV ??? = = = = >	0.0841

Key	Display
n	2
i	8.04 (two-year zero coupon rate)
PV ??? = = = = >	0.0771

Add the PVs together (0.0841 + 0.0771) and subtract from 1.00 gives 0.8388. That is the PV of the 1.09 we will receive in *three* years, but at what discount rate?

Key	Display
n	3
PV	−0.8388
FV	1.09
i ??? = = = = >	9.1246

Therefore, the three-year point on the zero coupon yield curve is set at 9.1246% p.a.

Using the same method the four-year point will be 10.2768.

Thus our zero coupon yield curve will be as follows:

Year 1	7%
Year 2	8.04%

Year 3   9.1246%

Year 4   10.2768%

4.9.7   Specimen trading strategies and yield curves

How can yield curves be used to advantage?
There are a number of ways in which a play on the yield curve can be used to advantage. These strategies are nearly always connected with yield differentials between different maturities. These ideas will also lead to further appreciation of what a good understanding of financial arithmetic can mean.

Riding the yield curve
A fairly simple strategy based on a positive yield curve, which is static or gradually steepening. Buy a 91-day Treasury Bill, at a yield of say 12.41 priced at 97.00. Two months later, when three-month bills are still yielding about 12.41 but one-month (30-day) bills yield 11.67% sell the bill as a one-month instrument for a price of 99.05. For an investment of £100,000 nominal value, this will pay:

Pay	− 97,000.00
Receive	+ 99,050.00
Profit	+ 2,050.00

Thus we have made £2050 on an investment of £97,000, in a two-month period of 61 days.

$$2050/97,000 \times 100 = 2.1134\%$$

$$2.1134 \times 365/61 = 12.6458\% \text{ p.a.}$$

This provides us with a yield which is greater than holding the original bill until maturity.

Alternatively:

A second strategy is the classic mismatch deposit trade whereby profit can be made on a negative yield curve, by for instance issuing a bond with a five-year maturity to fund short-term money market lending (e.g. 6-month Libor) at much higher rates.

The danger with most yield curve plays is that the yield curve will change in shape, i.e. a positive to negative change in the previous example is a recipe for losing money. Additionally, the yield curve may stay the same shape generally, but trade at a completely different level. There are trades that can take advantage of such expectations.

The answer may well be to take the speculative position and immediately hedge the outcome, using futures or FRAs.

A third strategy can make use of a flat yield curve. Say three-month (92 days) £ Libor/bid is 13.125–13 and six-month Libor (183 days) is also at that level. The forward view of rates is that broadly speaking they will remain at the same relative levels for the next three months.

There would seem to be little to be had in mismatch trading in the ordinary sense. Using a forward–forward play will produce an extra gain.

The objective is to produce funds at a cost below 13%, for future use.

From the above rates, using a forward–forward calculation, borrowing for six months at market Libor 13.125 (183/365) and placing funds back at the market bid (13.00%) (92/365) for three months only, we arrive at a forward rate for Libor 3 months in three months' time of 12.83%, a saving over spot 3-month Libor of almost 30 basis points. If we can lend at Libor in three months' time at the same level as today (remember we expect rates to stay stable), we have a locked-in funding cost of 12.83% p.a.

The risk: where will Libor 3 be in three months' time?

As a further refinement we could of course seek to hedge the 12.83%.

There are many other speculative plays involving yield curves in Swaps, Futures, FRAs and cross-market strategies. Yield curve plays in the main are not arbitrage, because they involve an element of position taking and therefore risk.

4.9.8 Adjustments for inflation and the premium for risk

The yield or return on any security needs to take account of inflation and risk. Adequate recompense for both is essential for a real return on investment.

All yield-bearing investments, deposits, bonds and shares, have to compete with each other and with consumption. Interest is the price of consumption forgone, and the goods and services which we consume are subject to inflation. In purchasing something to consume now rather than later, we eliminate both the effects of inflation and also the risk of default. In any security therefore, yield, however it is paid, must give adequate compensation for default risk and inflation.

Stripping out inflation from yield

If you wish to calculate the real return on an investment that pays a nominal yield of 16% p.a., when inflation is 9% p.a. you simply discount the nominal rate by the inflation rate:

$$\frac{1.16}{1.09} = 1.0642\%$$

$$= 6.042\% \text{ p.a.}$$

Thus our real rate of return is just over 6%. Note that, simply subtracting the inflation number is insufficient.

In everyday terms, it is justified as follows:

You need to buy a table for your new house. You have the choice of buying one at £100 now, or holding on to your money (and investing it) and paying £105 in a year, the £105.00 table being particularly good value.

If you invest the £100 now for a year, what rate of yield would you require to be able to afford the £105.00 table in a year, if inflation is 10% p.a.?

With inflation at zero, then a rate of return of 5% would be sufficient. Thus:

$$100 \times 1.05 = 105$$

With inflation at 10%, however, the price of the table will be 10% higher in a year, that is it will be 105 × 1.10 = £115.50. Therefore the yield you would require on your £100 investment for it to realise enough cash to pay for the table will be 15.50%, (not 15%).

$$£100 × 1.1550 = 115.50$$

From this, we can see that it is not adequate to add inflation numbers to real rates of yield, to establish what nominal rates investors should seek. Similarly, it is not accurate to calculate the real rate of return on an investment, or real interest rates, by subtracting the published inflation number.

The correct procedure is to divide the nominal rate by the inflation rate as below:

Nominal rate = 15%

Inflation rate = 10%

Real rate = 1.15/1.10 = 1.0455.

Conclusion: the real rate of return under such circumstances is 4.55% p.a., and the inflation premium must be 15 − 4.55 = 10.45%.

The other question that often arises, from wage and salary negotiations particularly, is whether it is more accurate to use past inflation or expected future inflation numbers in these kinds of calculation. You will note that, as regards investments and the desired real rate of return, we have used the expected figure for the future period of the investment. Relying on past data for these purposes is a little like driving a car using the rear view mirror alone.

Return for default risk

We now turn to the question of risk. Can we apply the same mathematical principles to real rates of return, that not only take account inflation, but default risk as well?

Typically, how can we adjust a lending rate to take account of possible default? Statistics will play a part, giving us the normal rate of default for a particular class of borrower.

Let us tackle a simple example.

If you sell widgets at £100.00 each on credit, and on average, 2% of your clients default, you are getting only £9,800.00, instead of £10,000.00 for every 100 sold. By how much should you increase your prices, to ensure that you achieve £10,000.00?

$$10,000/9,800 = 1.0204$$

Thus if you charge £102.04 each you will achieve your income objective. This yield calculation is quite simply interpreted, by saying that you require to earn £10,000, for £9,800 returned.

In terms of yield, on a loan portfolio, with a default risk of 0.5%, what would be the rate of yield that would have to be charged over and above an average cost of funds of say 12%, to achieve the breakeven target yield for the loan portfolio?

$$1,000,000 \times 1.12 = 1,120,000.00 \text{ (target return of principal + interest)}$$

This must be obtained from 99.50% of the portfolio, the actual return would be based on 995,000.00.

$$thus \qquad \frac{1,120.000}{995,000} = 1.125628$$

Therefore, an average yield of 12.5628% should be achieved on the loans in the portfolio to make up for the default rate of 0.50%. This will then achieve the same return as 12% on £1,000,000.00.

The proof of this works as follows. Invest £995,000 for a year at 12.5628%:

$$AV = 995,000 \times 1.125628 = 1,120,000$$

$$the \ same \ as$$

$$AV = 1,000,000 \times 1.12 = 1,120,000$$

In summary the formula for calculating the rate you must seek from an asset, looks like this:

$$\frac{1.1200}{1.00 - 0.0050}$$

or

$$\frac{\text{Desired return}}{\text{Principal less default rate}}$$

Returning to the very first example and modifying:

What is the real return on an investment that pays a nominal yield of 16% p.a., when inflation is 9% p.a., with a default rate of 0.50%?

Step 1

$$\frac{1.16}{1.09} = 1.0642\% \text{ (risk-free rate without inflation)}$$

Step 2

$$1.0642 \times (1.00 - 0.0050) = 1.0589$$

Conclusion

The asset yielding 16% per annum nominal, has a real rate of return of 5.89% if inflation is 9% p.a. and there is a default rate of one half per cent.

Adjustments for other types of risk
The processes that we have used for adjusting yield numbers to take account of inflation can be used for other types of risk. Exchange risk for example.

If inflation eats away at our investment return, so can exchange rate losses. There is of course another side to the coin, in that exchange rate movements can provide the investor with gains as well.

The calculation is a simple one, in that the numbers are easy to manipulate. The difficulty with this question is what number do we use?

An example will demonstrate this.

What is the real return on an investment that pays a nominal yield of 16% p.a., when expected inflation is 9% p.a., currency exchange rates are expected to move against us by 2% with an expected default rate of 0.50%?

Step 1

$$\frac{1.16}{1.09} = 1.0642\% \text{ (risk-free rate without inflation)}$$

Step 2

$$\frac{1.0642}{1.0200} = 1.0433\% \text{ (risk-free rate without exchange losses)}$$

Step 3

$$1.0433 \times (1.00 - 0.0050) = 1.038117$$

Conclusion

The Foreign Currency asset yielding 16% per annum nominal has a real rate of return of 3.81% p.a. If *expected* inflation is 9% p.a., exchange rates are *expected* to move such that the home currency will be 2% stronger at the end of the full year and there is a default rate of one half per cent in this class of investment, which is *expected* to remain constant.

5 Bond yield calculations – I

5.1 The relationship of yield and price

The yield of fixed interest securities with similar characteristics will always be similar. Like any traded instrument or currency, if one moves too far out of line, then some form of arbitrage deal will take place to move the yield back into line. A 5-year 10% coupon bond priced at par yields 10%. A similar 5-year zero coupon bond would tend to yield much the same, but with no coupon would have to trade at a much lower price.

The majority of fixed interest securities are redeemed at par. A $1,000.00 10-year coupon bond will be repaid by its issuer at maturity, after 10 years for precisely $1,000.00. By definition this bond will pay a coupon at intervals, the amount is fixed at say 10% p.a.

At issue, if yields for bonds with 10 years to go to maturity (including those that perhaps were issued 5 years ago as 15-year bonds), are all at about 10% p.a. then the new bond will not be worth any more or any less than its face or redemption value.

It will trade at par, *price* = 100.00

If yields are generally higher for similar maturities:

It will trade below par, *price* < 100.00

If yields are lower:

It will trade above par, *price* > 100.00

From this we can conclude that the yield of a bond:

(A) Increases when its price falls

(B) Decreases when its price rises

For example a Eurobond:

Maturity	5 years
Coupon	7.125% p.a.
Redemption	100.00
Yield to Redemption	8.00
Price = = = = >	96.51 of 100%

i.e. EuroDm bond Face Value Dm100 trades at Dm96.51.

If yields in the Deutschmark Euromarket fall to 7.90%, then the coupon represents a better investment than before and the bond price will rise to 96.90.

There is less capital appreciation from 96.90 to 100 than 96.51 to 100. That part of the yield computation that is capital growth has therefore decreased. Yield itself therefore falls to 7.90%.

From this we must conclude that yield and price cannot move independently of each other, because they are, mathematically, completely linked.

A change in yield will therefore produce a corresponding change in the price of a bond. The degree of change for a given yield will vary with such things as the time to redemption. This is known as the volatility of the security and is a more advanced concept, to be considered later.

5.2   Current, flat or running yield

Sometimes called interest yield/income yield this is the simplest method of calculating yield. It is not a good guide to the true yield to maturity of a security, but it is a fair short-term measure of its return as it ignores any change in capital value.

A better guide would include at least accrued interest as this is included in the actual price paid.

It is defined as the coupon as a percentage of clean purchase price:

Formula:
$$CY = \frac{G}{CP} \times 100$$

where
CY = current yield
G = coupon
CP = clean price (excludes accrued interest)

Problem

What is the running yield of the following 20-year Gilt Edged Security, Price $112\frac{19}{32}$, paying a coupon of 12.00%?

Substituting

$$\frac{12.00}{112.59375} \times 100$$

$$= 10.66\%$$

5.3 Simple yield to redemption

Generally, this measure of yield is less than ideal also, for two reasons. First it assumes a uniform capital growth ($+$ or $-$) during the life of the bond and secondly, it does not take into account the compounding of all coupon payments.

This method of calculating yield is frequently used in the domestic Japanese market.

Formula:
$$SY = \left[\frac{G + \left(\frac{100 - CP}{ym} \right)}{CP} \right] \times 100$$

where
SY = simple yield

G = annual coupon

CP = clean price

ym = years to maturity

i.e. coupon plus annualised proportional growth as a percentage of clean price.

Problem

What is the simple redemption yield of an 8-year bond with a 0% coupon, price 66.00 redeemed at 100.00?

Substituting

$$SY = \left[\frac{0.00 + \left(\dfrac{100 - 66}{8} \right)}{66} \right] \times 100$$

$$= 6.44\%$$

Thus we have implied steady growth from 66% to 100% of face value over a period of 8 years. Any coupon would be added to this and then expressed as a percentage of the purchase price.

For comparison purposes, $66.00 invested in a money market deposit at a yield of 6.44% for 8 years, would realise:

$$FV = 66.00 \, (1 + 6.44/100)^8$$

$$= \$108.74$$

The lack of compounding of income/interest makes a significant difference of $8.74.

5.4   Gross Redemption Yield

Gross Redemption Yield (GRY), Yield to Maturity (YTM) and

Redemption Yield are all synonyms for a method of calculating the value of a bond that overcomes the problem of compounding effect.

To understand Gross Redemption Yield, we need a clear understanding of how the price of a bond is calculated. The price of a bond is the sum total of all its cash flows, discounted to their Present Value. In other words, all the future coupon payments and the final redemption value (normally 100%) are all discounted to today's value and added together.

(The "Present Value" concept was covered in an earlier section of the manual, when compounded, discounted values were also studied.)

The formula used was the yield to discount or Present Value given yield, formula, and this is central to the whole concept of YTM or GRY.

$$PV = FV\left(\frac{1}{(1 + (i/100))^n}\right)$$

where

PV = Present Value
FV = Maturity Value
n = number of compounding periods or coupon dates
i = periodic yield to maturity

Important note

You will note now that the symbols used match four of the keys on the HP12C. The fifth of the 5 key set, "PMT" represents the amount of any coupon PAYMENT.

To be consistent, we will look briefly at the manual method of calculating GRY/YTM, merely to prove that the n, i, PV, PMT and FV key sequence is accurate.

Problem

A 7.00% three-year annual coupon bond, as defined by the AIBD rules, should yield 7.00% exactly, when it is priced at 100.00% or at par. Prove it.

$$PV = FV \left(\frac{1}{(1 + (i/100))^n} \right)$$

where

PV = Present Value
FV = Maturity Value
n = number of compounding periods or coupon dates
i = periodic *yield to maturity*

1. Discount each future cashflow to Present Value *at the target yield*, the example takes coupon *two*:

$$PV = 7.00 \left(\frac{1}{(1 + 7.00/100)^2} \right)$$

$$= 7.00 \times 0.873439$$

$$= 6.11$$

Year	Cashflow	Discount Factor	Present Value
1	7.00	0.934579	6.5421
2	7.00	*0.873439*	6.1141
3	7.00	0.816298	5.7141
3	100.00	0.816298	81.6298
		Price:	100.00

Conclusion: the price of a 7.00% coupon bond of whatever maturity, at a yield of 7.00% p.a., will be 100.00%.

Points to note

The discount factors used are all based on the GRY, "i".

The only further complication is that "n" will be a non-integer for fractional coupon periods. This is covered later. Adjustments will have to be made for semi-annual bonds, in that coupon periods will not be in years, but half years, i.e. the final periodic yield to maturity will have to be doubled for the final annual figure.

The calculation of *price* given GRY/YTM is fairly straightforward. However, solving for "i" in the equation above is usually done by a process of iteration. That is, the calculation GRY from a given *price* involves choosing a "ball-park" figure of GRY and seeing how close the resulting price is to that quoted, then adjusting the GRY estimates and doing it all over again until you finally get the quoted price. The GRY figure you used will then be the yield of the bond, with that price.

The HP12C procedure

After all the maths, you will be relieved to know that the HP12C procedures are very simple, provided you remember the significance of periodic GRY ("i" key) and coupon payment relationship ("PMT" key). This has arisen in basic compounding theory already and will be reinforced here.

Let us return to the earlier problem first and prove our long-hand calculation using the HP12C.

Problem

A 7.00% three-year annual coupon bond, as defined by the AIBD rules, should yield 7.00% exactly, when it is priced at 100.00% or at par. Prove it.

Key	Display
n	3
i	7
FV	100
PMT	7
PV = = = = >	− 100.00

Solving for PV (Present Valve = Price) the price of our bond proves to be 100.00.

You are now equipped to solve a number of problems, relating to any fixed-interest security, with a number of whole coupon periods until maturity, whether the coupon is annual, semi-annual, or quarterly.

Using the TVM keys allows indefinite "what if" exercises to be performed. (TVM = Time Value of Money.)

The next few examples relate to Eurobonds (annual coupon annual compounding).

Leaving the earlier figures in the calculator, change the yield to maturity (in "i") to 8.00. What happens to the price?

Key	Display
n	3
i	**8**
PMT	7
FV	100
PV ??? = = = = >	−97.42

By simply keying in 8 over the top of the 7 (which it replaces), pressing PV again gives the price you would pay to pick up an increased yield of 8.00%.

Try changing some of the other variables, but bear in mind that you cannot solve for "n".

You are given information about a bond investment as follows:

Term to maturity	5 years	(n)
Yield to maturity	8.12	(i)
Price	112.10	(−PV)
Redemption	100.00	(FV)

What is the coupon?

[answer 11.16% annual]

NB: Make sure you enter PV as a negative [CHS key] because you pay out cash for the bond. If you do not you will suffer from endless "Error 5" messages which seem to afflict us all when we are learning. Don't be discouraged!

You are an investor in a "zero" as follows. These are bonds which pay no coupon, or have had their coupons "stripped". In either case the original bond is sold at a deep discount, so that all income is made up of capital growth. This may be advantageous to high-rate income tax payers who pay little or lower rates of capital gains tax. A stripped bond will be sold at a discount, so that the yield is less than the original coupon, giving a profit differential.

Term to maturity	7 years	(n)
Coupon	0.00	(PMT)
Redemption	100.00	(FV)
Price	66.00	(−PV)

What is the effective cost to the borrower of raising capital in this way?

Solve for "i"

[answer 6.12% p.a.]

NB: Enter PV as negative (avoids "Error 5" again), because you are investing.

6   Bond yield calculations − II

The next stage is to look at bonds other than Eurobonds which have annual coupons and use a GRY/YTM calculation which involves annual compounding.

6.1   The calculation of bond yields having semi-annual coupons, compounded semi-annually

The best known of this type is the US Treasury Bond, mentioned already in earlier chapters. You have already seen how to convert US Treasury to Eurobond basis and vice versa, but this will all be summarised again later in this section.

The T-bond is a US Government bond. It pays a coupon twice a year and maturities range from 15 to 30 years. They are purchased by investors at auction, who bid a yield. The lower the bid the better for the government borrower, the higher the bid the better for the investor, but the chances of the bid being successful in competition are less. Thus successful bidding has to compromise yield. These securities trade in the secondary market on price, as distinct from yield. The following three HP12C procedures take account of this.

Problem

A US Treasury Bond with a 15-year maturity and a coupon of 6.55% is trading at 97.00.

Assume redemption value (FV) 100 (always the case for US T-bonds).

What yield does this represent?

The following procedure can be used for any semi-annual coupon bond with yields calculated on a semi-annual compounded basis.

Key	Display
n	30
PMT	3.275
PV	-97
FV	100
i = = = = >	3.436825 (periodic yield to maturity)
2 × = = = = >	6.87 p.a.

Points to note

The number of interest periods is twice the number of years to maturity. Hence 15 years is doubled to 30 interest periods.

The coupon rate of 6.55% per annum must be halved to its six-month cash value (the periodic coupon).

The final answer from the basic procedure must be doubled to achieve the redemption value per annum.

The HP12C being an American calculator, has a built-in program which we can use to calculate redemption yield. The advantage with this procedure is that it can be used with fractional coupon periods, i.e. when a bond is trading between coupon dates. The theory of fractional coupon periods will be covered later in this section.

The procedure uses the calendar function so make sure that the date format is set up to suit your requirements (D.MY or M.DY). We will use Day Month Year.

First of all we will use the program to prove the last example using the n, i, PV, PMT and FV keys.

Note that we are about to prove that the procedure using keys used for Eurobond GRY calculations (but allowing for semi-annual coupons), also works for T-bonds as well. Note also that T-bonds work on act/act day-year basis and Eurobonds, on 360/360. This has no effect, because the time fraction is always 1 when we are working with whole coupon periods.

Problem

A US T-bond with a 15-year maturity and a coupon of 6.55% is trading at 97.00. All T-bonds redeem at par 100%. What is the yield of this bond?

Information Settlement date: 1.06.1990
Maturity date: 1.06.2005 (or any 15-year date difference)

Key	Display
PMT	6.55
PV	97
1.061990	ENTER
1.062005	
f YTM = = = = >	6.8736%

Note that none of the cashflows needs signs, the redemption value is already programmed in and the final yield does not need to be doubled. Always use 6 decimal places for dates.

This program can obviously be used for odd dates, and it can be used for UK Gilts, Japan Government Bonds and any others that have a semi-annual coupon, paid on an act/act basis. The sequence can be altered to solve for price, given a known yield, as well.

What will be the price of a T-bond, yielding 8.25, given the following?

Coupon 8.125
Settlement 1.05.1990
Maturity 1.04.2000   (note the odd dates)

125

Key	Display
i	8.25
PMT	8.125
1.051990	ENTER
1.042000	

f PRICE = = = = > 99.1532

The price will be 99.1532. Note that this is a decimal, prices of T-bonds are normally quoted in 32nds. It is also what we call a clean price, in other words, there is no accrued interest included, which must happen before final settlement.

We can, however, include this quite easily at this stage, if we were to calculate what it should be. The coupon is 8.125% therefore as the bond is one month past its last coupon date (on the anniversary of its redemption), it has accrued 30 days' interest.

6.2 Accrued interest

Simple interest

Key	Display
PV	100
n	30
i	8.125
f INT	
R↓	
x > < y = = = = >	67 cents

This can be added to the clean price of the bond for settlement.

Alternatively, we can key in the sequence above for finding the clean price:

Key	Display
i	8.25
PMT	8.125
1.051990	ENTER
1.042000	

f PRICE = = = = > 99.1532

then key R↓ = = = => 0.67

This means that the calculator automatically calculates the accrued interest which is then added to clean price.

It is perhaps worth spending a little time explaining why accrued interest is added to clean price, or why accrued interest is sometimes negative.

When a bond is bought (or sold), accrued interest is always included in the "dirty" price; "clean" price only equals "dirty" price on a coupon date, with no accrued interest. If I were to sell you a bond which paid a coupon one month ago, then the bond I am selling will already have accrued one month's interest, to which I am entitled.

I sell it to you for a clean price. In 11 months' time (Eurobond) you cut out the coupon and send it to the paying agent for the issuer, who will pay you a full year's interest. I am, however, entitled to one month of that, because I owned the bond for a month before selling it to you. Thus, in selling it to you for its clean price, I have lost the interest. The dirty price thus should include all the accrued coupon; in this case accrued interest for one month.

Some bonds go ex-dividend, like a UK Gilt Edged Stock, some 37 days before coupon date and accrued interest becomes strangely, negative; in other words the dirty price is lower than the clean price.

The reason for this is that if I sell to you a Gilt some 10 days before the coupon date, I will calculate 10 days of *negative* accrued interest. This is added (it is negative) and the clean price falls. Why do you pay less?

The answer is that as far as the Registrar of Gilts is concerned (the Registrar maintains the bond-holder's register and unlike Eurobonds these are not bearer securities), he thinks that I still own the bond, because it takes more than 10 days to change the register. I will therefore receive all the interest at the next date, including the last 10 days of the year to which I am not entitled. Hence I sell, deducting those 10 days from the price.

6.3   Fractional coupon periods

With the exception of calculating redemption yields using the HP12C's built-in program, we have only considered the concept of whole numbers of coupon periods remaining in the life of a bond. To summarise this, every cashflow, coupon and redemption payment is discounted to Present Value using the established formula we are familiar with.

$$PV = FV \left(\frac{1}{(1 + [i/100])^n} \right)$$

where

   PV = Present Value
   FV = amount of future periodic coupon
   i = assumed periodic yield
   n = number of coupon periods

If a bond is purchased between coupon dates, it will be necessary to compound the fraction of the coupon period left over. This is done by adding a decimal fraction to the integer index number "n" in the formula above.

For example
An 8% annual coupon Eurobond has a yield of 8% with four years six months to maturity. In six months' time, there is a coupon payment of $8.00.

$$PV = 8.00 \left(\frac{1}{(1 + [8/100])^{0.50}} \right)$$

$$= \$7.70$$

This is currently worth $7.70.

In 18 months' time there will be another coupon of $8.00.

$$PV = 8.00 \left(\frac{1}{(1. + [8/100])^{1.50}} \right)$$

$$= \$7.13$$

This is currently worth $7.13.

If we carry on, tabulating each cashflow as follows, we come up with the price of the bond, in terms of the present value of all its cashflows.

Year	Cashflow	Present Value
0.50	8.00	7.70
1.50	8.00	7.13
2.50	8.00	6.60
3.50	8.00	6.11
4.50	8.00	5.66
4.50	100.00	70.73

Total of the Present Values gives a price of 103.93

This is a dirty price, because it includes $4.00 accrued interest. The clean price should thus be 99.93. This might seem a little strange. Surely an 8% coupon bond, yielding 8% should trade at par. The reason for this is that the calculation has relied upon a fractional index number (0.50) for the first half year's accrued interest. From earlier chapters, we know that normally we use simple interest, that is the actual number of days over 360 for Eurobonds, which will produce a small difference. The conventions used in fractional indices compounding mean that compounding is actually daily during the fractional period.

Note on periods using the HP12C calculator

The use of odd periods in the n, i, PV, PMT and FV keys with bonds is best avoided. Whereas some calculations appear to work, involving simple interest, such as on loans, which work on the actual number of days in an interest period, the calculations on bonds can be very misleading. It is probably safer to avoid the problem or use the program set out in the manufacturer's handbook.

The HP19B in this respect is safer, but care is still needed and users of the HP19B will note that the results of the tabulated calculation above (using a Eurobond sequence), reproduce the same numbers exactly.

6.4 Reinvestment risk

All fixed-rate bond yield calculations assume, for compounding purposes, that all coupon payments will be reinvested at the original yield of the bond, when purchased or sold. This is because all the cashflows are discounted at the same rate to achieve the price of the bond.

Year	Cashflow (coupon)	Discount Factor (at a 7% yield)	Present Value of cashflows
1	7.00	0.934579	6.5421
2	7.00	0.873439	6.1141
3	7.00	0.816298	5.7141
3	100.00	0.816298	81.6298
		Price:	100.00

Conclusion: the price of a 7.00% coupon bond of whatever maturity, at a yield of 7.00% p.a., will be 100.00%.

Thus a bond priced at par with a coupon of 7% will only yield 7% if all interim payments of interest are reinvested at 7%. This of course may not and probably will not, be possible. Although the coupon of a fixed interest security will not change during the life of the security, the price of the bond, and therefore its yield, will change. You obviously cannot guarantee the rate for reinvesting all the future coupons. This is the interest rate risk that investors suffer, if they invest in coupon bonds, whether they are held in portfolio until maturity or not.

Problem

A 10% annual coupon five-year bond priced at $107.98 is purchased with a yield to maturity of 8.00%. Before the next coupon is paid the yield to maturity drops to 7.00%. What happens if the reinvestment rate is only 7.00%?

Year	Cash Flow	FV at end year 5
1	10	13.11 [4 years after payment]
2	10	12.25 [3 ,, ,,]
3	10	11.45 [2 ,, ,,]
4	10	10.70 [1 ,, ,,]
5	10	10.00 [paid at end of year 5]
5	100	100.00 [paid at end of year 5]
		157.51

At maturity in five years from now, the first 10% coupon paid after one year, reinvested for the remaining four years will be worth 13.11 with full compounding at 7.00% p.a. The second reinvested at the same rate of yield for three years, 12.25 and so on.

Key

n	4	3	then falling 2,1 etc.
PV	-10	-10	etc. continued
i	7	7	etc. continued
FV =	13.11	12.25	etc. and so on
			to a total FV of 157.51

Conclusion

The total value of the investment at maturity, including the redemption of the bond and all the reinvested coupons is 157.51, from an original investment of 107.98. This growth takes place over five years and therefore the final annual rate of yield is computed as:

$$\frac{[157.51]_{0.20}}{[107.98]} - 1 \times 100$$

$$= 7.84\% \text{ p.a.}$$

Compared to the original yield on purchase of 8.00% p.a. i.e. annualised percentage growth of the *total* investment from purchase price (107.98) to redemption (157.51) is the fifth root of the five-year rate of 45.8698%.

Note: it is simple enough to substitute in "i" any reinvestment rate for any period or periods and assess the return on a steadily falling reinvestment rate for example. If the reinvestment rate continues to fall, the yield from the investment will therefore continue to fall.

Such exercises are best performed on a spreadsheet, which allows the indefinite substitution of different yields. The way to do this is to construct a table as outlined above.

6.5 Certificates of Deposit with multiple coupon periods

Introduction

Having already covered Certificates of Deposit with single coupons, payable at maturity together with the principal sum invested, it is logical, having covered compound interest and bond yields, to examine the methods for calculating prices and yields on CDs with more than one coupon.

Variable coupon periods, but fixed coupon

The normal bond yield calculation always assumes that coupon periods are always the same length. With CDs this is not the case, because interest is always calculated on the actual number of days in each coupon period. In a given year, for example, the first period might be 183 days long and the second 182 days. This means that we cannot use conventional bond mathematics to calculate its price and yield.

Modus operandi

The principle we use is to start at the far end, the maturity date of the CD, and identify how many days there are in each coupon period, right back to today. We then take the maturity value of the CD (100%) plus accrued interest for the final period and discount this back to the *penultimate coupon date.* Add the accrued interest payable at this point to the discounted figure you have and then discount all of this, back to the previous (*ante-penultimate*) coupon, using the number of days in between.

An analogy which comes to mind is that of a curtain rail with evenly spaced rings or sliders on it. The curtain is closed from left to right. When you draw open the curtain from the right (far) end you collect the last ring which collects the next one, which in turn collects the next one along and so on until you have them all together at the left or near end.

There is no short cut for these calculations. Computer software will of course be able to contend with the complexity, but the manual version is unavoidably protracted. However, use of the HP12C in an intelligent way will speed up the process and enhance accuracy.

Example

You have a two-year CD with three coupons left, paying 14% per annum, face value £1,000,000.00. How would you price this with 83 days to the next coupon (or after 100 days from issue), with current yields at 13 7/8%?

C_{today}	C1	C2	C3
nil	83	182	181

Discount the total value at point C3 back in time, 181/365 days to point C2.

Total value of CD at C3 is £1,000,000 + interest of £69,424.66.

Key	Display
n	181/365
i	14
PV	−1,000,000
FV = = = = >	1,069,424.66

This calculates the accumulated value of principal and interest from C2 to C3.

Key	Display
13.875	i
PV	1,000,579.96

This is the current PV of the total final value of principal and interest. For safekeeping, STO 0 will store the result.

Next, using simple interest, establish the accrued interest for coupon period 2 (182 days long) payable at C2. This works out at £69,808.22. Add this to the present value at C2, of C3, £1,000,579.96. This gives £1,070,388.18.

Key	Display
1,070,388.18	FV
182/365	n
13.875	i
PV = = = = >	1.001,125.39

So, the present value of cashflows at C3 and C2 but at point C1 is £1,001,125.39.

All we now need to do is to add this to the interest that would accrue in point C1, of 83 days plus 100 days already accrued. This is £70,191.78, giving a total value at C1 of £1,071,317.17. This is now discounted back to today, by 83 days at 13.875.

Key	Display
1,071,317.17	FV
13.875	i
83/365	n
PV = = = = >	1,038,549.51

The price of the CD is £1,038,549.51.

An alternative method, which is no less protracted, is to discount the value of each cashflow at its point C(x) back to today and adding the total present values. This cashflow at point C3, being £1,069,424.66 is discounted 181 + 182 + 83 days to today and so on. This can be more or less as cumbersome.

7 Floating rate securities

The mathematics of floating rate securities is arguably made more complex by the fact that the return to investors/issuers is mainly a coupon linked to an index which changes – sometimes semi-annually, occasionally quarterly and rarely more frequently – such as six-month Libor, reset monthly.

For the purposes of this manual it will probably be easier to think in terms of a margin over Libor as a positive margin and a margin under Libor as a negative margin over Libor.

The index will be typically Libor (London Interbank Offered Rate), Pibor (Paris), Mibor (Madrid) and many more. ECU issues relate to Eibor which is European Interbank Offered Rate, since the ECU is not a national currency. The index therefore is quoted on a money market day-year basis.

The instruments involved, which in mathematical terms are identical, but may differ in terms of credit risk, are Floating Rate Notes and Floating Rate Certificates of Deposit. There are also odd complications such as Variable Rate Notes (VRNs).

Yield evaluation methods

The main methods of evaluating yields on floating rate securities are as follows:

1. Effective margin – simple method
   – compound method
2. Current marginal income

Note the significance of the word margin. All floating rate securities linked to an index are concerned with the *margin* over or under that index.

Position evaluation

1. Implied Coupon Date Price

In addition, we can evaluate a position using what is known as Implied Coupon Date Price, which is self-evidently a price-based evaluation of a current holding in FRNs against the price in the market for that security, coupled with the money cost of carrying the position. It is a way of marking to market a floating rate investment.

7.1 Effective margin

7.1.1 Simple method

Effective margin is the total marginal return over the index, to maturity. It is a combination of margin (negative or positive) over the index, plus capital growth or depreciation.

For example:

$$\text{Margin} + \frac{[\text{Redemption Value} - \text{Price}]}{[\text{Life}]}$$

Life: 10 years
Margin: 25 basis points over six-month Libor
Price: 98.50
Redemption: 100

Using the calculator:

Key	Display
0.25	
ENTER	enters margin
100	
ENTER	enters redemption
98.50	
—	total capital growth from purchase to redemption

10

÷   per annum capital growth

+ = = = = = >   0.40

Thus the *simple effective margin* is 40 basis points

This number can then be compared with similar bonds as a basis for evaluating an investment. The factors that will affect the simple effective margin are those that appear in the calculation. Margin over the index, which is governed by credit strength and rating of the issuer. Clean price, again a reflection of the quality of the issuer and the demand for the paper in the market.

The simple effective margin is increased (decreased) by a larger (smaller) margin over Libor, thus with a VRN this will change after original issue, but will not change in a conventional FRN. The factor governing simple effective margin, after an FRN has been issued and thus its margin over the index fixed, will be price. As price falls, so the margin increases and as price rises, so it falls.

7.1.2   Compound method

The simple method for calculating effective margin can be compared to the Japanese method for calculating the yield on a fixed interest security, in that neither takes into account the present value of future cashflows in the bond. Compounding is not therefore a feature of the calculation.

Using the bond calculator, you can reach a sound result by inventing one notional fixed interest bond with a coupon the same as Libor, trading at par. It will yield the same as its coupon.

Take a second notional fixed interest bond with a coupon the same as Libor plus the FRN margin, trading at the same price as the FRN. Calculate the yield on this security. Now, calculate what the difference in the yields is between the two bonds. This is the effective margin, which takes compounding into account.

Worked example

For the sake of the example we will assume six-month Eurodollar Libor to be 8%, the FRN details remaining the same as the earlier example:

Life:	10 years
Margin:	25 basis points over six-month Libor
Price:	98.50
Redemption:	100

Notional Fixed Rate Coupon – Bond I

Coupon:	8.00%
Price:	par 100
Redemption:	100
Maturity:	10 years
Yield:	8.00%

Notional Fixed Rate Coupon – Bond II

Coupon:	8.25%
Price:	98.50
Redemption:	100
Maturity:	10 years
Yield:	?????

Using the calculator:

Key	Display
n	20 (the coupon is semi-annual, we are linked to six-month Libor)
PV	−98.50
PMT	4.125 (half Libor plus 1/4 margin)
FV	100
i = = = = >	4.2377 × 2 = = = = > 8.4754%

$$8.475 - 8.00 = 0.475$$

The effective margin on the FRN is 0.475%.

Once again, this is a method of evaluating an investment proposition. The factors that will affect the effective margin (compound method) are likewise, price and margin over the index. As price falls so yield rises and consequently margin rises and vice versa.

7.2 Current marginal income

The number for current marginal income represents the annual income from the floating rate security that you derive, after taking into account funding your holding at Libor. It is a simple spread figure, the difference between the cost of an investment over time and the benefit from it.

It is calculated as follows:

$$(\text{Libor} + \text{FRN margin}) - (\text{price} \times \frac{\text{Libor}}{100})$$

If, as before, Libor is 8.00 and the price of the security is 98.50 then substituting:

$$8.25 - (98.50 \times 0.08) = 0.37\%$$

Therefore current marginal income is 0.37% p.a. for this security.

The factors that affect, decrease or increase, the CMI of a floating rate security are the price and therefore the cost of the investment in the first place. This is governed by supply and demand for the paper in the market place. In addition, the margin over the index will affect the spread over the cost of carrying the investment in portfolio. The margin, as before, is a matter of credit perception, by the issuer and his advisers. If this is too low in the opinion of the investor, then price will be affected.

The conclusion that we can draw from this, is that the deeper the discount of the bond price and the higher the Libor, the higher will be the marginal income, even with the same margin over Libor. The margin will not normally change during the life of the bond, so the measure becomes price dependent.

$$10.25 - (98.50 \times 0.10) = 0.40\% \text{ p.a.}$$
$$8.25 - (97.50 \times 0.08) = 0.45\% \text{ p.a.}$$

7.3 Implied coupon date price

What is ICDP?

If you purchase a floating rate security today, using Libor cost funds, the coupon date price is the price level at which the security must be sold, to break even. It is a method for marking to market the current holding in a particular security.

The formula for calculating this is a little complex but can be broken down into its component parts.

$$\text{Price} + \frac{\text{Price} \times \text{Days 1} \times \text{Cost/Funds}}{360\,(365) \times 100} - \frac{\text{Coupon 1} \times \text{Days 2}}{360\,(365)}$$

Price = gross price paid for security
Days 1 = days from settlement to next coupon
Cost/Funds = cost of funds for same period
Days 2 = days in coupon run
Coupon 1 = current coupon

$$\text{Price} + \frac{\textit{Price} \times \textit{Days 1} \times \textit{Cost/Funds}}{\textit{360 (365)} \times \textit{100}} - \frac{\text{Coupon 1} \times \text{Days 2}}{360\,(365)}$$

The section of the formula in *italic*, is the total cost element of the investment, the non-italic, the reward for holding it. The difference between the two, the ICDP, is what you must achieve at the next coupon date, to break even. If you can do better, you profit, or worse, you incur a loss.

Substituting the following values:

Currency: US dollar (US Money Market basis)

Coupon: 8.25%

Libor: 8.00%

Purchase settlement date: 25th May 1990

Last coupon: 20th May 1990

Next coupon: 20th November 1990

Price: 98.50

1. Gross price

Dirty price = clean price + accrued interest (6 days, 20 to 25 May)

$$= 98.50 + \frac{5 \times 8.25}{360}$$

$$= 98.6146$$

2. Cost of carrying FRN to next coupon date

$$\frac{\text{Price} \times \text{Days 1} \times \text{Cost/Funds}}{360 \times 100}$$

$$= \frac{98.6146 \times 179 \times 8.00}{36000}$$

$$= 3.92$$

3. Less coupon to be received at next coupon date

$$\frac{\text{Coupon 1} \times \text{Days 2}}{360}$$

$$= \frac{8.25 \times 184}{360}$$

$$= 4.22$$

Conclusion

$$98.6146 + 3.92 - 4.22 = 98.31$$

The implied coupon date price is currently 98.31

From these calculations, we can observe that the factors that affect ICDP and thus the profit and loss position against the market price of the particular holding are:

1. The purchase price of the security which has to be carried (funded).
2. The cost of funding the purchase, current Libor or index.
3. The coupon, which will be a combination of Libor or index when the coupon was last set, plus the margin. The Libor or index may be different from the *current* cost of funding if they do not coincide as above. If cost of funding is cheaper, this will obviously lower the ICDP needed to make a profit.

8 Annuities and amortising front-end fees

8.1 Annuities

Introduction

An annuity is any financial structure which will achieve an output result for a given number of input cashflows during its life, assuming a certain rate of yield. For example, you might buy an annuity with a lump sum, which you have inherited, which will give you a certain income each month for the next five years, until principal and interest are used up. Or, if you have a son or daughter to educate, you might invest a sum of money when they are born which, at a rate of yield guaranteed by the fund manager, will provide you with a tri-annual payment for school fees, until the fund is exhausted. These are typical annuities as are most house mortgages and amortising loans. The common factor with any annuity is the exhaustion of the principal, even if this involves a final payment to clear the balance.

On the HP12C, annuities can very simply be worked out, using the n, i, PV, PMT and FV, in almost any combination.

The most important part of the technique of constructing and evaluating an annuity, is to plan the cashflows, making sure that you have the direction correctly signed, with pluses and minuses. Borrowings consist of positive cashflows from the drawdown, followed by a series of negative cashflows, to repay principal and interest. Loans (as viewed by the lender (assets) and investments, consist of a negative cashflow for the cash invested and positive cashflows for the sums paid by the investment, including repayments of principal.

Let us suppose that you have inherited a sum of $50,000. You contact your investment adviser about the annuity to boost your income over the next five years. She calculates that for $50,000 you could receive a monthly income of $943.56 starting at the end of one month. What sort of yield is this and how was it worked out?

These steps will demonstrate the technique; note the use of the blue "g" key before the "n" key inputs the five years as 60 months.

Key	Display	
g "n"	5	(inputs 60 months in five years into n)
PV	− 50,000	(invest your 50,000)
PMT	943.56	(amount of monthly income)
i ??? = = = = >	0.416661	
12 × = = = = >	5.00	

Thus the yield is 5% p.a.

The conclusion from this is that if you invest $50,000 now, you will, at an assumed yield of 5% p.a., receive a monthly income, of principal and interest, of $943.56, at the end of every month for the next five years, until funds are exhausted.

The same annuity structure can be used as a savings plan.

You decide to save £50 per month for the next 20 years for your well-earned retirement and you estimate that the interest rate available to you will average about 6% per annum after tax. How much will you have to spend in 20 years' time?

Key	Display	
g "n"	20	(240 months)
g "i"	6	(6% p.a. but paid as 0.50% per month)
PMT	− 50	(*Negative* cashflow, *investing* £50 per month)
FV = = = = >	£23,102.04	

You will receive £23,102.04 in 20 years' time, compared with investing 240 × £50 per month, a sum of £12,000.

Leaving the keys undisturbed, it occurs to you that you have £1500 on deposit at the moment. What would the result be if you boosted the investment with a lump sum at the beginning?

Quite simply, key 1500, CHS, PV and then solve FV again. The result is £28,067.35 with fully compounded growth, that is interest *must* be left in.

Loans of various types often have annuity structures, and you borrow and repay over time, both principal and interest until the loan is fully repaid.

Amortising loans

Take a five-year loan, for US$10,000,000 at a rate of interest of 8% p.a., repaid over that time, with both principal and interest. What would the repayments be?

Key	Display	
PV	10,000,000	(inputs amount of loan)
n	5	
i	8	
PMT = = = = >	− 2,504,564.55	

We can say that if we borrow US$10,000,000 for five years, then the repayments will be US$2,504,564.55 each year for five years.

We can obtain more information from the calculator than this, however; we can obtain, quite readily, the breakdown of principal and interest in each of these payments. We know from simple interest calculations that the interest on US$10,000,000 in year 1 will be US$800,000 and thus principal repaid will be (2,504,564.55 − 800,000) = 1,704,564.55.

We need not work this out because we have it available already.

Recapping the earlier key strokes:

Key	Display
Key	**Display**
PV	10,000,000 (inputs amount of loan)
n	5
i	8
PMT = = = = >	− 2,504,564.55

Now key

n	1
f AMORT = = = = =>	− 800,000 (the *orange* n key function)

We get − 800,000 which you will recognise as the interest. Now press R↓ and the figure of $1,704,564.55 appears, which is the proportion of principal you repaid in year one. RCL PV gives you the amount of principal remaining.

If you now key 1 into "n" again and press f AMORT again, you get $663,634.84, and R↓ gives you $1,840,929.71. This is interest and principal paid/repaid the second year.

If after keying in the first four lines again (down to solving the PMT number), you key in 5 into "n", and f AMORT, you will obtain the total interest paid over 5 years (US$2,522,822.73) and R↓ confirms that you will have repaid $10,000,000 also.

The ability to be able to split each payment into principal and interest is important; for example, for tax purposes, if tax relief is allowable on the interest element.

Further refinements

We can adapt, almost infinitely, the structure of our loan. In the previous example, if we preferred to have the loan structure changed so as to allow repayment of US$5,000,000 as a partial bullet at maturity, then we would key:

Key	Display
PV	10,000,000
N	5
i	8
FV	−5,000,000 (repayment of half the principal as a "bullet")
PMT	−1,652,282.27 (repayments during the loan are reduced)

This may be a more acceptable means of funding a project, where income from it is expected later in its life. As far as the lender is concerned, the level of yield of the asset is maintained at 8% p.a.

8.2   Annuities due

All the earlier situations change if the timing of the payments change; let us return to the theme of your retirement which we looked at earlier.

You decide to save £50 per month for the next 20 years for your well-earned retirement and you estimate that the interest rate available to you will average about 6% per annum after tax. How much will you have to spend in 20 years' time?

Key	Display	
g "n"	20	(240 months)
g "i"	6	(6% p.a. but paid as 0.50% per month)
PMT	−50	(*Negative* cashflow, *investing* £50 per month)
FV = = = = >	£23,102.04	

This is an ordinary annuity; you are making your investment month by month, but at the end of those months. What would happen if you invested your money at the *beginning* of the month?

On the face of it, you would think that making all your investment payments earlier than before, would mean that they earn more interest because they are invested for longer. You would be correct in your assumption.

You decide to save £50 per month for the next 20 years for your well-earned retirement and you estimate that the interest rate available to you will average about 6% per annum after tax. How much will you have to spend in 20 years' time, provided you start immediately and pay in your £50 at the *beginning* of each month?

First of all you will need to adjust the calculator. After clearing the calculator, key "g" and the "7" key, which you will note has the word "BEGIN" on it in blue. The word also appears in the display. The machine is now set to beginning mode.

Key	**Display**	
g "n"	20	(240 months)
g "i"	6	(6% p.a. but paid as 0.50% per month)
PMT	− 50	(*Negative* cashflow, *investing* £50 per month)
FV = = = = >	£23,217.55	

Instead of receiving £23,102.04 in 20 years' time, you will receive £23,217.55. Not a big advantage, but the cash pay-out is improved for a given yield as expected.

8.3 Front-end fees on bond issues and loans

Introduction

This section examines the change in yield produced by incorporating front end fees on bonds, option premiums on interest rate caps, and arrangement fees on term loans. While these fees may be quite clearly stated at the time the business is transacted and the fee paid, it is rather more useful to know what the effect on the bottom line yield figure will actually be. This means not only spreading the cost over the life of the asset/liability, but including the cost of carrying the fee, which was paid up-front, over the whole life of the transaction.

For example, if you borrow money for five years and invest in an interest rate cap (a means of setting a maximum interest cost of a loan), it might cost 2.50% flat of the principal sum, payable at the beginning of the loan. You might be tempted to say that the payment of this "premium" will add 50 basis points to your cost of borrowing each year (2.50/5). This ignores the fact that you must "carry" the cost of the hedge throughout its life, because you paid up-front.

The calculations to give a full cost are very similar to any yield to maturity calculation (as set out in earlier chapters) and use the n, i, PV, PMT and FV keys on the HP12C. (Reset to g "END".)

Problem

A typical fixed-rate New Zealand dollar issue due 1st October 1993 (three years).

Details   Coupon: 17.125

Issue price: 101.625

Yield: 16.40 gross

16.84 less selling concession (1%)

Amortisation: Bullet

First of all, for a little practice, we will compute the bond yield and look at some basics of bond issues.

Key	Display
PMT	17.125
PV	− 101.625 (use the CHS key)
FV	100
n	3
i ??? = = = = >	16.40

Bringing in the selling concession (deducting it)

RCL
PV = = = = >   −101.625

1

+   (removes selling concession)

PV

i = = = = >   16.84

Conclusion

The issue could be sold as cheaply as 100.625 when the selling concession is taken into account. This sales incentive allowed by the issuer
raises the overall yield to the borrower, to 16.84. In practice, the
borrower expects to pay 16.84% and the drop in price to 100.625 lowers
the profitability for the syndicate of banks in the issue. What in effect
has happened is that the selling concession of 1% of the face value of the
bond adds 44 basis points to the yield to the borrower.

8.4 Front-end premium of an interest rate cap (Libor-based)

Much the same sequence is used to calculate the additional annual yield
that paying a single front-end premium creates, when a cap is purchased. Either the bank selling the cap will require a single front-end fee,
or if the cap is investor-provided, the Libor-based coupon will have to
be increased by extra yield to compensate for capping. (A cap is an
option to limit interest payable on a security, with a number of
coupons.)

Problem

An issuer of an FRN in US dollars over five years buys a cap which is
set at a level of 9 per cent per annum. The FRN is indexed to six-month
Libor which is currently at 7% p.a. The front-end fee for the cap is
1.36% flat. What does this add annually, to the yield?

Key	Display
FV	-100
n	10
PMT	-3.50
PV	$(100 - 1.36)$ (inputs the principal sum, less the cost of the cap)
i × 2 = = = = = >	7.33%

The additional cost of the cap is 33 basis points on top of the initial coupon rate of 7%.

Conclusion

This is ultimately an identical calculation for a semi-annual 7% fixed income bond, priced at 98.64, redeemable at 100 in five years' time.

The HP12C allows indefinite "what if" exercises, so it is a simple matter to change the coupon rate to perhaps 8%, to assess what the effect will be on the amortised cost of the cap (34 bp at 8, and 35 bp at cap rate). You will observe that the rate at which the fee is amortised is a question of judgement. The fee is paid out at the front end of the transaction. As it therefore has a cost of carry over the life of the transaction, is it acceptable to amortise at the same rate? Would it be better to amortise at the cap rate since this is the worst scenario? You will also observe that the effect on the annualised figure of selecting different rates is very small.

Note: the assumption has been made that the cost of the cap will be amortised at 7%. If a different rate is used, then this should be entered in PMT as a negative divided by two for semi-annual coupons and amortisation.

As an alternative, the calculation can be carried out without involving the bond structure.

The earlier example quoted a 9% cap priced at 1.36% of principal sum, amortised at the Libor index of 7%. It added 33 basis points per annum to the cost.

Key	Display
PV	-1.36
n	10
i	3.5
PMT $===\;=>$	0.163528
$\times 2 ====\;>$	0.33

This is a tidier way of computing the cost and the cost of carrying the premium of 1.36% can be varied as required. By changing the "i" to 4.50, and recalculating PMT, we get 0.171875, doubled to annualise, giving 34 basis points. There are slight differences in the different methods, but don't lose sight of the practicalities. It is not worth spending thousands in expensive salaried time to be accurate to the "n^{th}" decimal place, when the market is not concerned with such accuracy. More to the point perhaps is the figure at which the fee is amortised. This will change from day to day and the calculation might well be different tomorrow. The important thing is to have a *reasonably* clear idea of the additional cost of hedging a position.

9 Internal Rate of Return

Internal Rate of Return (IRR) is one of the more important tools for finance managers. It is used in project finance and risk management extensively and is an extremely useful technique. It is based on the same principles that we have covered in the arithmetic of fixed interest securities although it is rather more versatile. Simply, it provides a yield figure for a series of cash flows or somethimes a series of financial instruments, such as might be used in hedging certain types of interest rate risk.

9.1 Definition

IRR, as it is usually known, is the rate at which all future cash flows in an instrument or transaction must be discounted, to reach the present value of that instrument or transaction.

It may be compared with ordinary Yield to Maturity, Gross Redemption Yield and Yield to Redemption, but it is a more versatile measure of the characteristics of an instrument because it takes account of uneven cashflows, including nil payments, but all on regular dates.

The calculations involving the HP12C use the following keys:

> g CFo, CFj and Nj for input purposes

> f IRR to execute the calculation

As with many other calculations we have done using the HP12C, IRR is sensitive to cashflow direction and thus we must carefully analyse the direction of each cashflow in terms of pluses and minuses, otherwise errors will result, which either will render the calculation unworkable or, more dangerously, will work but give an incorrect answer.

154

The basic IRR calculation will usually only involve one change in direction of the cashflows. Typically you invest and then receive your rewards later, or you borrow and repay afterwards. With complex projects, such as those that require investment of funds for a number of years, then a period of cash withdrawal followed by a further series of investments, followed by yet another series of cash payouts, two changes of direction result and the IRR calculation needs to be treated with more care. Having said that, the basic IRR calculation is usually sufficient for most needs and it is quite sophisticated enough.

9.2 Comparison with Gross Redemption Yield

Problem

Calculate the GRY of a Eurodollar Fixed Rate Bond with three years to redemption paying interest annually at 8% p.a. on a 30/360 day-year basis, priced at 105.125 (redeemed at 100%).

Recapping YTM calculations using n, i, PV, PMT and FV:

Key	Display
PV	− 105.125
FV	100
PMT	8
n	3
i ??? = = = = >	6.0799% p.a.

Now, recalculating using the IRR sequence demonstrates the similarity between the two. What is the point if they are so similar?

IRR calculations will provide a yield to maturity value for any series of cashflows, however uneven in amount they are, provided they are chronologically regular.

Key	
− 105.125	g CFo
8	g CFj

8	g CFj
108	g CFj

f IRR = = = = > 6.0799% p.a.

The result is identical with the previous calculation.

Points to note

1. The cashflows must be analysed correctly, especially the final one which includes coupon and repayment of principal. Cashflow signs *must* be used. Great care is needed to ensure data is input correctly, although correcting errors is fairly easy.
2. The repetitious input of coupon payments can be simplified either by hitting the g CFj keys the required number of times repeatedly inputting the coupon in the display, or more efficiently by using the Nj key as follows.

The next problem is designed to show how to avoid keying in repetitive cashflows one by one. The sequence involves the use of the "Nj" key.

Problem

What is the YTM of an eight-year 8% annual coupon bond, price 110.00 and redemption value 100.00?

Cash flow analysis shows a pattern of nine payments with the schedule below:

Year 1	−110.00 (1 payment)
Years 2–8	8.00 (7 payments)
Year 8	108.00 (1 payment)

This would be laborious to input individually (even more so if it was semi-annual), and uses up memory in the calculator. Again, so that we can check our IRR technique is correct, we could (and normally would) calculate the yield of a bond like this, using the n, i, PV, PMT and FV keys, because it is much simpler and quicker. For practice, therefore, calculate the yield as you have seen before. It should be 6.366221% p.a.

Using the IRR sequence should result in an identical number, even to the sixth decimal place:

Key

−110	g CFo
8	g CFj coupon rate
7	g Nj number of coupons excluding the final one
108	g CFj
f IRR = = = = >	6.366221% p.a.

What we have done here, after the first cashflow of −110, was to input an 8% coupon and by inputting "7" and "g Nj", to tell the calculator that there are seven of them. The final cashflow includes a coupon of 8% but this is part of the total 108.00, to be received at maturity.

Note: the number of different cash flows that can be entered using the g CFo and g CFj keys is 20. If there is a pattern or series of identical payments (e.g. coupons) this increases to 99 using the g Nj key.

9.3 Using the IRR function for uneven cash flows

Problem

We will use an unusual bond issue by Bergen Bank A/S., their Declining Coupon, US dollar Bonds 1986–1991. The coupons are tabulated alongside the year they are paid, declining from 10% in 1987 to 7 3/8 in 1991.

Coupons:

10	1987
8.375	1988
8	1989
7.50	1990
7.375	1991

Clearly the routine sequence we have used for yield to maturity will not work on a coupon payment structure such as this as it is completely uneven in size, but evenly spaced. What would we put into the PMT key for example?

We can now proceed to calculate the yield to maturity using IRR, assuming the issue price was 103.00 and redemption value 100%.

Cashflows:

Initial	− 103 (1986)
1	10 (1987)
2	8.375 (1988)
3	8.00 (1989)
4	7.50 (1990)
5	107.375 (1991)

Now, to input the information follow the key strokes overleaf.

Key	**Display**
− 103	g CFo
10	g CFj
8.375	g.CFj
8.00	g CFj
7.50	g CFj
107.375	g CFj
f IRR = = = = >	7.5976% p.a.

Our conclusion is that the yield of the bond is 7.5976, as it is trading over par, with a coupon which on a straight average is 8.25. The yield against the average coupon using conventional bond maths is 7.6087, which is close but not accurate.

At this point, given clearly identifiable, differing cashflows, we can consider changing data. What would the yield of the bond be if the first coupon was 9.00% not 10.00%? Clearly it will be lower. Now, note from the information above that the 10% coupon is cashflow 1 after the *initial* cashflow. If you RCL 1 you will see 10.00 on the screen and that is where the calculator stored the data that you input first, under g Cfj. RCL 5, shows you 107.375, the last cashflow. Now STOre another number, such as 9.00 in STO 1.

Key STO 1, followed by f IRR, and after a pause, we have the new yield to maturity, of 7.37. RCL n tells you how many cashflows there are, RCL i shows the yield again and so on.

The next problem shows us how to deal with cashflows which do not exist. These cashflows may be for a nil amount, but we must take account of them. For example, we may encounter a situation, in project finance for example, where a series of cash payments are made to finance a project. When these cease, we enter a period in which cash paid in equals cash paid out, a nil net cashflow. Later still the project pays out cash profits. We must take these "nils" into account if we are going to get an accurate result.

To illustrate this we will use an unusual bond, which paid no interest for five years and then paid the accrued simple interest at 8.50% for those five years. Finally, two conventional coupons were paid.

Problem

B.N.P. 8.50% 1986–93 US dollars.
This bond pays simple interest at 8.50% after five years and then two 8.50% coupons after that.

Coupon: 42.50% after five years followed by 8.50% p.a. in 1992 and 1993.

Cashflow as follows:

−100.00	1986
0	1987
0	1988
0	1989

0	1990
42.50	1991
8.50	1992
108.50	1993

Assuming the bond is trading at par, calculate the yield.

Key	Display	
− 100	g Cfo	
0	g CFj	
4	g Nj	(four years at this level)
42.50	g Cfj	
8.50	g Cfj	
108.50	g Cfj	
f IRR = = = = >	7.5861% p.a.	

Conclusion

The coupon value for four years is zero. Nevertheless, this must be entered, otherwise the sequence represents a bond with a single payment of 42.50% in year one, 8.50% in year two and 8.50% plus 108.50 in year three only.

Final notes on error messages

It is possible that you have occasionally encountered an "Error 7" message; well done if you haven't! This message merely tells you that there is no answer for the data you have input. Probably you will have made an error like forgetting a minus sign somewhere, so that all cashflows go in the same direction.

9.4 Zeros

The IRR function can also be used with zeros, which we have already encountered in passing. These are bonds which are issued without coupons, or whose coupons have been stripped, that is removed and traded as individual, but smaller zero coupon bonds in their own right. They trade at a deep discount. Thus yield is entirely made up of capital growth, with no year-to-year income. To a high-rate tax payer, subject to little or no Capital Gains Tax, this may be an advantage.

Problem

What is the yield to the issuer of an eight-year Japanese yen zero coupon bond, trading at 66.00% redeemable in eight years at 100.00%? (Euro-bond annual compounding.)

Key	Display
66.00	gCFo
0	gCFj
7	gNj
-100	gCFj ("includes" the final (8th) zero coupon)
f IRR = = = = >	5.33%

This can be proved using the n, i, PV and FV keys (PMT = 0) because the coupon cash flows are all identical (nil) and usually if you wish to work with zeros, these are the keys you would use. Nevertheless it proves that IRR will work for most regular cashflows, even nils, but you must give the calculator all the data.

9.5   The difference between YTM and IRR

Broadly speaking there is no difference between Yield to Maturity/Yield to Redemption/Gross Redemption Yield and Internal Rate of Return, except that IRR is much more versatile.

An investor tends to look at the YTM of a bond; a portfolio manager, financial engineer or syndicate manager involved in creating a financial package with multiple cashflows for a client borrower, would tend to look at the IRR of the package, with all things taken into consideration.

IRR can also be used to price up certain types of swap and futures transactions, amortising structures in loans (and swaps to cover them) strip structures, such as Futures strips, series of Forward Rate Agreements, Caps and the like.

9.6   Net Present Value

Introduction

Net Present Value (NPV) is a recognised decision-making tool for project investment. It can be a method of assessing the current profitability of a financial structure when the costs of funding it change. NPV, which is different from, but often confused with, PV or present value, is actually a differential between two PVs. The difference between a PV obtained at one rate of discount and the PV obtained at a different rate of discount.

Given a project, like a business expansion, using borrowed monies, we can measure the present value of the investment, at the rate of yield we would like to see and at the rate of yield we are actually achieving. We will obtain two sets of present values, the difference is NPV.

We know that if we discount a series of cash flows at a rate of discount D we will get a particular PV, called P. If we discount them at a higher rate than D, say D+ then our PV will fall to P− (like bonds, as yield rises so price falls).

If P was what we wanted and P− is what we get, we can say that our NPV is negative, a lower value. A rule of investment in anything is that if the NPV of a project is negative, it is not worth the investment. Thus if funding yields in our expansion project rise, we can, using NPV techniques, exactly quantify the damage it does to our project's viability. It can be used as a measure of the project's sensitivity to interest rate risk.

Example

We have the following project structure, with projected cashflows over the next five years as follows:

Year 1 invest £10,000,000

Year 2 invest £10,000,000

Year 3 break even

Year 4 receive £10,000,000

Year 5 receive £20,000,000

We seek a high return from this project because we need to cover funding costs of some 12%, a figure that we can guarantee by means of an interest rate swap, with a profile to match the project cashflows. Question, will we make a profit in the first five years or not?

Using the IRR key sequence, shown earlier (the gCfo and Cfj sequence), *with* cashflow signs we can answer the question:

Key	Display
− 10,000,000	gCfo
− 10,000,000	gCfj
0	g Cfj
10,000,000	g Cfj
20,000,000	g Cfj

We now have all the data we need, so input the target rate of 12%, cost of funding, key 12 i.

Now key f NPV (the PV key). The figure of 899,592.62 appears, which as it is positive tells us that our project is viable.

Now key f IRR and we have 13.65% IRR, the actual rate of return we are getting.

The final conclusion we can draw is that the £899,592.62 is the current excess value of the project, over its costs. If you like, the project is worth £899,592.62 more than we are investing at today's values. It might, for example, represent the present value of the accruing surpluses or profits over the next five years. In terms of interest rate risk too, the NPV number has value. If the rate of financing was not fixed at 12.00%, but floating, we could measure precisely what the effect would be on NPV of a rise in the funding cost. At some point where the positive NPV threatens to turn negative, but still at reasonable cost, we could hedge our interest rate risk.

10 Cashflow creation

10.1 Even cashflows

There are areas of the banking and finance industry where it is desirable to create certain cashflows, to meet particular future commitments. The Swap market relies on the creation of even cashflows to fund the fixed side of a fixed/floating Interest Rate Swap. These cashflows are relatively simple to create, by purchasing the appropriate fixed interest security such as a US Treasury, in the absence of a matched trade. The use of one transaction, matching another with dissimilar cashflows, but similar yield is a way of hedging risk.

The valuation of these cashflows is straightforward and has been covered in the Chapter Nine on Internal Rate of Return and Redemption Yields etc.

10.2 Uneven cashflows

The creation and valuing of future unequal but regular cashflows is important in other engineered finance packages, where for example fund managers need to invest cash to meet specific future obligations, minimising risk of loss. The use of fixed interest securities can be material in creation of the desired annuity to provide the necessary future cashflow.

An understanding of the principles of Discounting and Internal Rate of Return is an integral part of the correct design and performance measurement of the portfolio.

Problem

We will take a relatively simple problem, involving small amounts, but the principle obviously holds good for larger amounts with greater numbers and complexity. It may be a relatively simple problem super-ficially, but you will note that the complexity quickly builds up.

You require the following cashflows over the next five years. The question is how much will it cost to create them today? Five-year yields are currently at 12%.

Total investment: ??

Dollar returns required each year:

Year 1	$110
Year 2	$120
Year 3	$130
Year 4	$140
Year 5	$110

Available bond yields are:

5 years	12.00%
4 years	11.00%
3 years	10.00%
2 years	9.50%
1 year	9.00%

The following principle will apply to any future set of uneven cashflows.

Cover the final year first ($110 required)

Buy five-year bonds which realise principal and interest at redemption totalling $110. Given five-year yields at 12%, then any investment which realises a final cashflow of $110 will suffice and we will choose as follows. If we buy bonds, priced at a cost of $98.21, then as this throws off cashflows of $11.79 each year (including the last year) then an IRR calculation will demonstrate that such a structure yields 12%. Clearly there is an almost infinite number of cashflow structures that will yield 12%.

We have:

Yield	Initial cost	Yr 1	Yr 2	Yr 3	Yr 4	Yr 5
12%	98.21	11.79	11.79	11.79	11.79	(11.79+98.21)=110

This series could, for example, be produced by buying $98.21 of par bonds, with coupons of 12%. 12% of $98.21 is $11.79 and final redemption (at par) brings in $98.21 plus the final cashflow of coupon income of $11.79.

Cover the penultimate year next ($140 required)

Buy four-year bonds which realise principal and interest at redemption of $140. Once again we have to look at what is available in the market place. Four-year bonds yield 11% p.a. We can work backwards as before but note that we already have a $11.79 cashflow each year. So in year four we actually need $140 − 11.79 = $128.21. Once again we find that if we buy bonds that yield 11% each year for the next four years, and if they cost $115.50 they will throw off coupon income cashflows as follows:

Yield	Initial cost	Yr 1	Yr 2	Yr 3	Yr 4	Yr 5
11%	115.50	12.70	12.70	12.70	(115.50+12.70)=128.21	

The arithmetic is a little complex so we will examine further how we arrive at these numbers.

We can use the n, i, PV, PMT and FV keys on the HP12C. The arithmetic is exactly like buying a single (if rather unusual) bond that redeems at a dirty price of 128.21. including a coupon of 12.70% (redemption value must therefore be 128.21 − 12.70 = 115.50).

If we enter a structure like this, it yields 11% p.a.

Key	Display	
−115.50	PV	(cost of bonds)
4	n	(term)
115.50	FV	(redemption value)
12.70	PMT	(coupon income)
i = = = = >	10.9957%	

To illustrate this further, it is rather like buying $115.50 *worth* of bonds priced at 100 (par) they must pay a coupon of 11% the same as the yield, so the coupon of 11% of the invested sum of 115.50 is $12.70 in coupon income. They then redeem at par, repaying the invested sum of $115.50 plus a final coupon with a cash value of $12.70, total $128.21.

Now we continue on in this way until all cashflows have been created.

Schedule

% gain on amount invested

Yield	Initial cost	Yr 1	Yr 2	Yr 3	Yr 4	Yr 5
12%	98.21	11.79	11.79	11.79	11.79	110.00
11%	115.50	12.70	12.70	12.70	128.21	
10%	95.92	9.59	9.59	105.51		
9.5%	78.47	7.45	85.92			
9.0%	62.82	68.47				
	450.92	110.00	120.00	130.00	140.00	110.00 (610.00)

Using the IRR program in the HP12C, you will see that the yield on this is exactly 10.8377%.

Key	Display
−450.92	g CFo
110	g CFj
120	g CFj
130	g CFj

140	g CFj
110	g CFj
f IRR = = = = >	10.8377

For practical purposes, the fund manager can say at this stage, that this structure will yield 10.8377% p.a. over the next five years. Reinvestment risk is absent because the coupons are not reinvested; their resultant cashflows are used to provide the desired sums (perhaps to meet maturing insurance policies) at the various yearly intervals. The fund manager has used this structure in the same way as a series of zero coupon bonds.

As an exercise, if you were to discount all of the total annual cashflows at the rate of 10.8377, and then add them together, you would arrive at a present value of 450.92 – the original cash cost of the bonds.

11 Coupon stripping

While considering the further use of the Yield to Discount formula, we can look at an interesting way in which the calculation is used in an arbitrage-like trade, in bonds. This is coupon stripping. The practice of coupon stripping represents an alternative way of making profit in capital market instrument trading.

How it works

What actually happens is that a bond, such as a US Treasury Bond, is purchased for a price. The coupons are "stripped" off, and then sold separately as zero coupon instruments in themselves and the bond, bereft of its coupons is now a "zero" and is sold also.

The arbitrage difference that arises to create the profit comes from reselling each coupon and the bond itself at a price commensurate with its position on the yield curve. We know that a bond is the sum total of the present values of its cash flows, all discounted at the (same) yield of the bond, perhaps the four-year yield. When the coupons are stripped off and sold individually as one, two, three and four-year "bonds" in their own right, they will be priced off the yields for one, two, three and four-year instruments. These will almost certainly be different, but the art is to find a favourable difference. In practice, of course, the coupons themselves need to be large enough to trade in, as zero coupon bonds.

Example

A 12% five-year Eurodollar Bond is purchased at 100.91, yielding 11.75% p.a. The yield curve is positive, with rates for maturities from one to five years as follows:

Year:	1	2	3	4	5
Yield:	10.00	10.50	11.00	11.50	11.75

Cashflows:

Year	Amount	Yield	Disc Factor	Present Value
0	− 100.91			− 100.91 (price paid out)
1	12	10.00	0.9091	10.91
2	12	10.50	0.8190	9.83
3	12	11.00	0.7312	8.77
4	12	11.50	0.6470	7.76
5	12	11.75	0.5738	6.89
5	100	11.75	0.5738	57.38
				101.54 (price received)
			Profit	0.63

Conclusion

The individual components are priced like zeros and sold off separately for their present values, like individual zero coupon bonds, instead of all being discounted at the yield rate for the original bond. Total received 101.54 against an initial cost of 100.91; the difference is a locked-in profit. The principal difficulty likely to be encountered is the sale of the coupons, because, as zero coupon bonds, they have very small values and may be difficult to get rid of. The term arbitrage-like is used, because the sale of the various components may take some time and the "simultaneous" nature of an arbitrage is hard to achieve, thus the term is stretched a little.

12 Measures relating to yield − I

In addition to Running Yield, Simple Yield to Redemption and Gross Yield to Redemption (or Yield to Maturity), there are other measures of yield used for other instruments, such as loans, or bonds with sinking funds. GYR is not used for loans, but some measure of the way an asset like a loan behaves is important, so that risk may be managed and the effective life of the asset measured. These further measures are:

− Average Life
− Yield to Average Life
− Yield to Equivalent Life
− Equivalent Life

Yield to Maturity is a fair measure of a bond's value only if the bond is held to maturity, but with the acceptance of reinvestment risk. This is somewhat unrealistic. An investor may very well part with an investment early. Some bonds, and of course, term loans as well, are redeemed or repaid earlier than final redemption date, using a schedule of repayments, a redemption schedule, or what is known as a "sinking fund".

For a bond with a sinking fund, proportions of the outstanding issue are redeemed on specific dates, at predetermined values, set at the time of issue. Cashflows can thus be determined in advance. The bond numbers are usually picked at random and published in the press, often as pages and pages of numbers in small type, which must give proof readers a headache. This early redemption of some of an issue causes problems when it comes to measuring the life of the bond. Thus initially some form of average is used, not unnaturally called Average Life.

12.1 Average Life

Average Life and its associated measure, Yield to Average Life, is an alternative measure to Yield to Maturity.

Problem

Given: 10% five-year Eurobond, price $107.99 has a YTM of 8.00%. (Check this for practice using the n, i, PV, PMT and FV keys.)

This bond has a sinking fund with a redemption schedule whereby 33.33% of the issue is redeemed after three years, 33.33% after four years, 33.33% after five years.

Bonds are normally redeemed at par 100.00%.

Anticipated cashflows are as follows:

Year	Redeemed	Coupon	Cashflows redemption	Total cashflow
1	nil	10.00	nil	10.00
2	nil	10.00	nil	10.00
3	33.33%	10.00	33.33	43.33
4	33.33%	6.67	33.33	40.00
5	33.33%	3.33	33.34	36.67

Average Life is a weighted average. It is defined in the bond context as:

The average redemption date weighted by the expected redemption cashflows.

$$\text{Average Life} = \frac{(3 \times 33.33) + (4 \times 33.33) + (5 \times 33.34)}{33.33 + 33.33 + 33.34}$$

$$= 4.00 \text{ years}$$

12.2   Yield to Average Life

The Yield to Average Life is then the yield produced by an equivalent bond with the same parameters but with the Average Life figure substituted for final redemption date.

To reiterate

Given: 10% five-year Eurobond, price $107.99 has a YTM of 8.00%.

Price: 107.99
Coupon: 10.00
Maturity: 4.00 (Average life (four years) substituted for final
                      maturity (five years))

Redemption: 100.00

Key	Display
FV	− 100
PMT	− 10
n	4
PV	107.99
i = = = = >	7.61%

Interim conclusion

The Average Life of the bond = 4.00 years
The Yield to Average Life = 7.61%

This will, to a degree, allow us to compare what we have with bonds of similar maturities and yields. This method does have an intuitive disadvantage, in that it does not consider the present values of the cashflows used. To overcome this problem we could resort to another measure which does. This is Equivalent Life and its associated measure, Yield to Equivalent Life. To look at this we will start with the associated measure, Yield to Equivalent Life first.

12.3   Yield to Equivalent Life

A question that might arise out of the previous calculation concerns the accuracy of the result, if we try to check it.

Let us return to the cashflow schedule and add another column:

Year	Redeemed	Coupon	Cashflows redemption	Total cashflow	PV at 7.60%*
1	nil	10.00	nil	10.00	9.29
2	nil	10.00	nil	10.00	8.64
3	33.33%	10.00	33.33	43.33	34.79
4	33.33%	6.67	33.33	40.00	29.84
5	33.33%	3.33	33.34	36.67	25.42
					107.99

* Note

You will note that the price of the equivalent bond, 107.99 only equals the sum total of the cashflows discounted at 7.60% not 7.61%. (At 7.60 the bond price would be 108.02.)

This indicates that 7.60% is actually a more accurate measure; it is called "Yield to Equivalent Life".

12.4   Equivalent Life

This is defined as:

> The weighted average of the redemption dates, weighted by the redemption cashflows, discounted by the Yield to Equivalent Life.

This differs from Average Life as the latter uses actual values rather than present values of redemption payments.

Yield to Equivalent Life can be easily, but monotonously, calculated by iteration, i.e. calculating and recalculating the sum total PVs using revised Yield to Equivalent Life numbers, until the price matches the market price of the bond. The final YEL figure used in the most accurate calculation is the correct figure. Thus in the example we used to calculate Yield to Average Life, we arrived at a figure initially, of 7.61%. If we then tabulated the cashflows, discounting them to their PVs at 7.61, we would have had a difference in price. The next step would be to change the yield and recalculate the table, until we finally got the price of the bond to agree with the total PV of the cashflows. This occurred at 7.60%.

There is not much difference between the two measures here and all the hard work of iterating might seem pointless; however, the further away from par that the bond is priced, the more significant the difference will become.

Equivalent Life can be calculated rather like Average Life but with the PVs substituted:

$$\frac{(3 \times 26.75^*) + (4 \times 24.86) + (5 \times 23.11)}{26.75 + 24.86 + 23.11}$$

$$= 3.95 \text{ years}$$

* **Note:** 26.75 is the PV of 33.33 discounted at 7.60% p.a. over four years.

Equivalent Life is always less than Average Life because the present values of redemption payments will always be less than their future value on payment.

13   Measures relating to yield − II

The foregoing section introduced certain methods of valuing bonds and other investments, having repayment or redemption schedules over a period.

These built on previous experience gained in using the Yield to Discount formula to calculate present value. The present value concept will continue to be important in the following section which introduces two further measures used in bonds:

1. Duration
2. Modified Duration (volatility)

13.1   Duration

Yield to Maturity is commonly used to measure the value of the life of a bond. This does not take into account the different timing of the various cashflows of different bonds. We have already encountered in earlier sections such things as graduated payment or stepped coupon bonds and bonds with sinking funds and explored ways such as IRR that can be used to calculate their yields.

Duration is a better method than YTM because it does take into account when cashflows take place. It can be defined as:

The average of the times of each cashflow, weighted by the present values of those cashflows.

From this you will see that Duration, measured in years, is similar to Equivalent Life, which only considers redemption payments. Duration considers all payments, including coupons. Duration is therefore an improved method of representing the way the price (or value) of a bond will behave.

Problem

Given two bonds:

1. A zero coupon six-year bond priced 58.00.
2. A six-year bond with a coupon of 10.00 priced at 102.21.

Calculate the Yield to Maturity of both bonds, using the n, i, PV, PMT and FV keys:

Key	Display
n	6
PV	-58
FV	100
i = = = = >	9.50%

Key	Display
PV	-102.21
PMT	10
i = = = = >	9.50%

Conclusion

Both bonds have an identical yield to maturity and should, if such a measure is to be relied upon, behave in the same way. Initially, as we have mentioned earlier, a coupon bond does have an inherent reinvestment risk; the zero does not. A zero coupon bond is immune from changes in interest rates provided it is held to maturity. But what happens if they are not held to maturity?

To illustrate these various points, we will take two bonds, 1 and 2. One a zero, the other a conventional coupon Eurobond, with annual compounding.

Bond 1. (The zero) delivers all cashflow in one payment of 100.00% at redemption, after six years, from a starting value (PV) of 58.00%, yielding 9.50%.

Bond 2. Delivers 10% coupons during its six-year life with a final

178

payment of 110.00 including the final coupon at redemption. Yield is also 9.50%.

A zero thus delivers its cashflows later in its life than does a coupon bond.

We will now compare them on the basis of Duration.

1. The six-year zero

Duration is simple to calculate on a zero; it is the same as final maturity.

A simplified formula will be useful here:

$$\frac{PVCFt \times Tn}{PVCFt} = D$$

where
$PVCFt$ = present value cashflow t
Tn = timing of cash flow in years, of the "n"th year, in this case year six.

Using the example above again, substituting

$$\frac{58 \times 6}{58} = 6.00 \text{ years}$$

There is only one cash flow with a zero: 100.00 at maturity.

2. The six-year 10%

This is a little more complex, because we need to consider all the cashflows. Using the formula again, but for each cashflow at each time interval, these can then be added together, and divided by the total present value of all cashflows discounted at the annual yield (the price).

$$\frac{PVCFt \times Tn}{PVCFr} = D$$

where
>   t = 1 to 6
>   n = 1 to 6
>   PVCFr is clean price of bond (present value cashflow
>   redemption)

Cashflow schedule: (YTM equals 9.50%)

Tn	CFt	PVCFt at YTM	PVCFt × Tn
1	10	9.13[a]	9.13
2	10	8.34[a]	16.68
3	10	7.62	22.86
4	10	6.96	27.84
5	10	6.35	31.75
6	110	63.81	382.86
		102.21	491.12

Next, take the sum of the (PVCFt × Tn) column and divide by the sum of the PVCFt column, which you will note is the price, PVCFr, thus returning to basic principles for a moment, is the YTM calculation.

$$\text{Duration} = \frac{491.12}{102.21} = 4.81 \text{ years}$$

Conclusion

The six-year zero bond has a Duration of 6 years.

The six-year coupon bond has a Duration of 4.81 years.

[a] **Note.** These two numbers, and those following in the same column are arrived at by discounting the coupons (each of 10) at a rate of yield of 9.50%:

$$10 \times \frac{1}{(1 + 9.50/100)^n}$$

where n is the number of years from today
>   i.e. $10 \times 1/(1.0950) = 9.13$ and $10 \times 1/(1.0950^2) = 8.34$ etc.

If, as we mentioned earlier, Duration is a measure of the way the value of a bond (its price) will behave, then these two bonds will not behave in the same way.

Duration can be used to improve hedging techniques. A trader may sell one bond in order to immunise a long position in another. He could try selling one with a similar YTM. We have demonstrated that it is quite common to have two bonds with identical YTMs to have quite different characteristics, the zero and coupon bond were one example. The hedge using one to immunise another, against changes in yield and price, as a result, will be imperfect.

Using Duration, which can be described as an index of the way the price of a bond will behave for given changes in yield, is a better measure which takes timing of cashflows into account and will provide better immunisation against adverse changes in yield. Specifically, two bonds with identical Durations, but different yields, can be used to hedge one another. We can, however, be more sophisticated; we can take two bonds, and construct a hedge, one against the other in a ratio, taking into account differing Durations resulting from different characteristics, with some success.

This means that we can hedge Government stock positions using a futures contract which differs from the stock being hedged. It means that we can hedge a five-year sterling Interest Rate Swap, using a six- or seven-year Gilt. Because we can link the cash position to the hedge in a ratio, relying on the Duration number, we can manage risk more safely. The detailed management of such risks is, however, beyond the scope of this handbook, which aims to inform in a user-friendly fashion how such measures as Duration are calculated. It is as well to note, that even given the benefits of Duration, two bonds with similar Duration may behave differently under certain circumstances and thus it would never be wise to set in place a Duration-matched hedge and then sleep on it. As with all hedges, it should be continuously monitored and adjusted if it becomes unacceptably inefficient.

What affects Duration?

Yield

Duration increases with increasing yield. (Try increasing the yield on the worked example and see what happens.) This is because the PVCF values fall with a higher discount rate, so your total present values divided by price are lower, along with the price itself, to a degree.

Maturity

The change in Duration due to change in maturity is more complicated, it will depend on whether a bond is trading above or below par, size of coupon and time to maturity itself. A simple rule that Duration increases with maturity will generally be correct in practice. There is a limiting factor, however, which affects Perpetuals and very long maturity bonds of 30 to 40 years. Here Duration actually starts to fall.

Coupon

A low coupon bond will have a higher Duration than a high coupon bond. The earlier example demonstrated that a zero (which is the ultimate in low coupon bonds) has the highest Duration, equal to maturity itself.

Duration analogy

Generally speaking, the later the cash payments are in a bond, the longer you have to wait for your money and the higher the Duration of the bond. This can be illustrated as follows.

Increasing yield means that the PVs of your coupons now are lower, so you have to wait for the value. Low coupon bonds mean that the price (PV) is lower now, so you have to wait for your value later. A zero coupon bond, with the highest Duration has no coupon so you have to wait full term for your money and so on.

Illustration

Take a straight, weightless plank of wood resting on a log. Place a number of buckets (assume these have no significant weight either) on the plank. The contents of each bucket represent the size of each cashflow, when it is paid. Five buckets represent a five-year bond. The point where the log produces a balanced position under the plank, represents the Duration.

With a five-year zero, you have to wait until year five to get all your money back; bucket five is full of water and the rest are empty. For equilibrium, the log must be positioned under bucket five and the Duration is therefore five (years).

With a low coupon bond, there are small cashflows (small amounts of water in buckets one to four) and the balance shifts to the left, just beyond bucket four. This corresponds to perhaps 4.30 years Duration.

According to the theory, as coupon rises, Duration falls. As the amounts of water in buckets one to four continue to rise, the point of balance shifts further to the left, to a position between buckets three and four. We have a Duration of 3.70 years.

13.2   Modified Duration (volatility)

Modified Duration is related to Duration by the formula:

$$MD = \frac{Duration}{1 + \left(\dfrac{Yield}{F \times 100}\right)}$$

where
      Y = Yield
      F = Frequency of coupon

It is a measure of the price volatility of a bond for a given small change in yield.

Thus the six-year 10% coupon bond priced at 102.21 will look like this:

Duration was 4.81. Yield 9.50 so:

$$MD = 4.81/(1.0950)$$
$$= 4.39 \text{ years}$$

This figure can then be proved using an example.

Change the yield by 1 basis point to 9.51.

The price changes from 102.21 to 102.1651, a move of 0.0449.

$$\frac{0.0449 \times 100}{102.21}$$

$$= 0.0440\%$$

The Modified Duration was 4.39 years, so for 1 basis point (0.01%) move in yield, we saw a change in price of 0.0440%, which is very close.

If yield changes to 9.60 (ten basis points, 0.10%), the price changes by 0.4473.

$$\frac{0.4473 \times 100}{102.21}$$

$$= 0.4376\%$$

Thus for bigger changes in yield the accuracy is less, but still a useful guideline and better than other ways to assess the behaviour such as Yield to Maturity.

As an additional example, we can look at a zero coupon bond.

Duration and Modified Duration of a zero coupon bond

Take a five-year, zero coupon bond, trading at 67.00%, which yields 8.34% p.a. We know that Duration is five years, the same as maturity, in a zero coupon bond. According to our earlier formula, the Modified Duration should be:

$$MD = \frac{Duration}{1 + \left(\dfrac{Yield}{F \times 100} \right)}$$

Thus

$$MD = \frac{5.00}{1.0834}$$

$$= 4.62$$

Now we can test this answer, by changing the yield by 0.01%, from 8.34 (actually 8.3391 to 8.3491) and see what happens. The price of the bond changes from 67.00 to 66.9689. A difference of 0.0311. How much is this as a percentage of the price?

$$\frac{0.0311 \times 100}{67.00}$$

$$= 0.0464\%$$

This is very close to the 0.0462% we were expecting from 0.01% change in yield. The measure is not totally accurate, but sufficiently so for normal purposes. For larger changes in yield, it becomes less accurate. In using Modified Duration for hedging purposes, it will be necessary to adjust the hedge periodically as the Duration itself changes.

In conclusion, we can say that if the Modified Duration of a bond is X, we expect the price of the bond to change by X times the change in yield, but for relatively small changes only. With Modified Duration of perhaps 6.82, we would expect the price of the bond to change by 6.82 × 0.01% or 0.0682% and so on.

Portfolio management

Duration and Modified Duration can be used for risk management in portfolios of bonds, as well as individual bonds. They form a useful measure of the way a portfolio behaves, for given small changes in yield.

A fund manager faced with a series of negative cashflows from maturing insurance policies over a period of time can immunise himself against interest rate exposure by making sure that he has a maturing investment every time, to meet a maturing policy. This may be safe but is practically impossible to do. To find a bond that matures on exactly the right date may not be possible. An alternative is to create a position with differing cashflows, but which *in effect* is the same. This amounts to matching the way your liability behaves in a market with the way your asset behaves. This is Duration-based hedging.

To assess the way a portfolio behaves with changing market conditions we can consider the Duration of a portfolio. This may be described as a weighted average of the individual Durations of the component bonds in the portfolio, weighted by their total present values. Even better, we can, once again, exactly quantify how a portfolio will change in value for given small change in yields. Portfolio Modified Duration is the tool used here.

An example using Eurobonds will illustrate this:

Coup-on	Mat-urity	Price	Yield	D	MD	NV	Cash value
10.00	3	102.5625	8.9879	2.74	2.51	5m	5,128,125.00
12.75	5	113.9375	9.1526	4.05	3.72	10m	11,393,750.00
11.50	7	109.7500	9.5283	5.26	4.80	3m	3,292,500.00
10.00	6	102.6250	9.4077	4.81	4.39	4m	4,105,000.00
							23,919,375.00

The total value of the portfolio is £23,919,375.00.

Calculating the weighted-average Modified Duration

The sum of (MD × cash value) for bonds one to four, divided by portfolio value, gives a figure of 3.7242 years. Intuitively this looks correct because in this case more of bond two is held than any other bond, and its Modified Duration is 3.72.

MD	Cash value	MD × Cash value
2.51	5,128,125.00	12,871,593
3.72	11,393,750.00	42,384,750
4.80	3,292,500.00	15,804,000

| 4.39 | | 4,105,000.00 | | | | | | 18,020,950 |
| | | | | | | Total | | 89,081,293 |

$$\frac{89,081,293}{23,919,375}$$

$$= 3.7242$$

From this we can deduce that the value of the portfolio will change by 0.037% for every 0.01% point change in yield of the securities within it.

Coupon	Maturity	Price	Yield	D	MD	NV	Cash value
10.00	3	102.5883	8.9779	2.74	2.51	5m	5,129,415
12.75	5	113.9798	9.1426	4.05	3.72	10m	11,397,980
11.50	7	109.8027	9.5183	5.26	4.80	3m	3,294,080
10.00	6	102.6700	9.3977	4.81	4.39	4m	4,106,800
					Revised value of portfolio		23,928,275

The final question is, by how much has the portfolio changed in value, for 0.01% change in the yield of each bond? According to our theory, by $3.72 \times 0.01\%$ or 0.0372%.

Original value 23,919,375
Revised value 23,928,275

Change 8,900

As a percentage of the original portfolio value

$$\frac{8,900 \times 100}{23,919,375}$$

$$= 0.0372\%$$

From this we can conclude that Portfolio Modified Duration, which is a weighted average of the Modified Duration of all the bonds within it, weighted by the cash value of the holding of each of the bonds, will give a reasonably accurate indication of how the portfolio will change in value for a small change in yield of each security.

The problem with this idea, which is appealing in concept, is that in practice it is difficult to use. The reason is that for it to behave perfectly, an absolutely parallel shift in the yield curve must take place, i.e. all the yields on the bonds in the portfolio must change up or down, by the same amount, regardless of their maturity and therefore their position on the yield curve. This is rather unlikely in reality.

The other disadvantage, and this applies to individual bonds as well as portfolios, is that as circumstances change, time passes, yields change, and prices move, so Duration and in consequence, Modified Duration also change. This means that we must always monitor anything, such as a hedge, which relies on these measures. We cannot simply calculate the figures and then sit back and assume they are constant. It is this factor which renders Duration and Modified Duration inaccurate for larger changes in yield, because as the yield changes so Duration and Modified Duration themselves change.

13.3   An introduction to Convexity

Duration will indicate how the price of a bond will change for small changes in yield and Modified Duration will give a reasonably accurate measure of the price response for a given small change in yield.

Under certain circumstances, it is possible for two bonds to have an identical Yield to Maturity, have a very similar Duration, but behave differently when larger changes in yield occur.

An alternative measure of a bond's response to larger changes in yield which overcomes this problem is the bond's Convexity.

What is Convexity?

If you were to plot Yield against Price for two bonds of identical YTM and Duration you would demonstrate that the bond with the higher Convexity moves higher in price, for a given fall in yield, than the bond with the lower Convexity. Conversely, for a given fall in price, the bond with the higher Convexity will move higher in yield than its lower Convexity alternative. The term Convexity is derived from the shapes of these plots, which as you would see, is curved. The bond whose data gives the curve with the smaller radius (the more convex shape), not unnaturally, has the higher Convexity.

There are a number of ways to calculate Convexity, but to calculate accurately the Convexity of a bond, the following formula can be used:

$$Cx = 10^8 \times \frac{1}{Pd} \times ([Pa + Pb] - [2 \times Pd])$$

where
        Pd = dirty price
        Pa = dirty price with 1 bp increase in yield
        Pb = dirty price with 1 bp decrease in yield

Note that the use of at least seven decimal places is essential.

Take a bond as follows:

Maturity: 10 years
Coupon: 8% annually
Yield: 12%
Dirty price: 77.39910788 (on coupon date)
Duration: 6.8374

Price at 12.01% yield = 77.35187731

Price at 11.99% yield = 77.44637871

$$Cx = 10^8 \times \frac{1}{Pd} \times ([Pa + Pb] - [2 \times Pd])$$

$$= 10^8 \times (1/77.39910788) \times ([77.35187731 + 77.44637871] - 2 \times 77.39910788)$$

$$= 10^8 \times 0.01292005 \times 0.00004022$$

$$= 51.96$$

The Convexity of the bond is 51.96.

For comparison purposes, we could take a similar bond:

Maturity: 6 years 301 days
Coupon: zero
Yield: 12%
Dirty price: 46.08293469
Duration: 6.8389

Price at 12.01% yield = 46.05481702
Price at 11.99% yield = 46.11107204

$$= 10^8 \times (1/46.08293469) \times ([46.05481702 + 46.11107204] - 2 \times 46.08293469)$$

$$= 10^8 \times 0.02170001 \times 0.00001968$$

$$= 42.70$$

The Convexity of the zero is 42.70 which is substantially different from the coupon bond, which has a very similar Duration and an identical Yield to Maturity. What this demonstrates is that although it would be safe to hedge a long position in the zero with a short position in the coupon bond, for *small* changes in yield, the zero will move further in price than the coupon bond for a *large* change in yield.

Convexity will therefore give us a more accurate measure for the way a bond will behave, for larger changes in yield, and allow us to hedge more effectively, since we are continually having to adjust our hedge, if several small changes take place, which in themselves are small, but cumulatively become quite large.

Convexity is also a useful indicator to the investor in bonds who, comparing the two we have just considered, still seeks out the bond which will move further for a given change in yield. On the face of it, the investor should be quite indifferent, since the Yield to Maturity is the same in each case and the Duration very close also.

In terms of Convexity, though, the coupon bond will give a measurably better price performance for the same change in yield.

III   Mathematics for Swaps

14 Long-term Swaps

General introduction

Any Swap may be regarded as the exchange, physically or effectively, of an instrument with one set of characteristics for an instrument with a different set of characteristics.

Example: the exchange of Japanese yen for US dollars for a five-year period – a Cross Currency Swap.

    or

The exchange of a fixed interest coupon payment stream for a floating interest rate payment stream, for five years – an Interest Rate Swap.

    or

A combination of both, fixed rate dollars swapped for floating rate yen – a Cross Currency Interest Rate Swap.

The whole subject of Swaps is surrounded by much myth and in some cases apprehension. The understanding of these instruments, which can indeed be complex, can also be simplified. Eliminate the awkwardness of adjusting semi-annual Swap rates to annual, eliminate the need to price a Swap based on a semi-annual bond, on an annual money-market basis and you have eliminated much of the problem. Up to now, you have explored many and complex structures by taking them apart in a logical way, examining their cashflow framework and evaluating them in terms of Yield, Present Value and Future Value. Swaps are no different.

A bond with its yield and price, its coupon and its redemption payment, is a series of discrete (as distinct from continuous) cashflows. A Swap is no different.

Forward Start Swaps, as we shall see, rely on basic compound interest for their pricing; Swap risk and Swap reversal calculations are nothing more than the simple annuities structures that we have already covered. With this in mind, much of the learning process can be made easier.

14.1 Cross Currency Swaps

General introduction

The Swap allows an institution to exchange an instrument with one set of characteristics for an instrument with a different set of characteristics.

A Currency Swap is generally an Interest Rate Swap first and foremost but involving two currencies, most of which have the US dollar on one side of the transaction. The technique allows a borrower of fixed rate yen to exchange the liability for fixed rate dollars, the borrower of floating rate Deutschmarks (Dm) to exchange for fixed rate dollars or for that matter, but more unusual, a borrower of fixed rate Deutschmarks to obtain access to fixed rate yen. In other words, the Cross Currency Interest Rate Swap, as one might call it, is fundamentally an interest rate hedging vehicle but with cross currency implications.

The major difference between the single currency Interest Rate Swap and the bi-currency Interest Rate Swap is that whereas principal amounts are never exchanged in the former they may be exchanged at the beginning of a Currency Swap, but must be re-exchanged at its termination.

For those participating in this market, the risks are correspondingly greater than conventional Interest Rate Swaps as there is an interest rate risk, with a currency position risk as well if default occurs. Most business is done on a matched basis to avoid excessive position risk, with greatest liquidity in the five- to ten-year range.

Example

A borrower ABC of fixed rate Dms, with US dollar income, has a fairly typical problem in liability management.

German interest rates are rising and dollar rates are falling, causing a weakening of the dollar. The borrower has a currency mismatch between income and expenditure.

By borrowing Dms, some time ago, while the currency was weaker against the US dollar and its interest rate was lower, the arrangement worked well. However, in order to hedge against increasing currency losses through the accompanying strengthening of the Dm, the borrower enters into a Swap, in which he pays floating rate dollar Libor, receiving fixed rate Dms in return.

In doing this, the borrower of fixed rate Dm has (a) hedged his currency risk and (b) unlocked his fixed rate of interest into floating dollar rates which are falling.

An illustration follows:

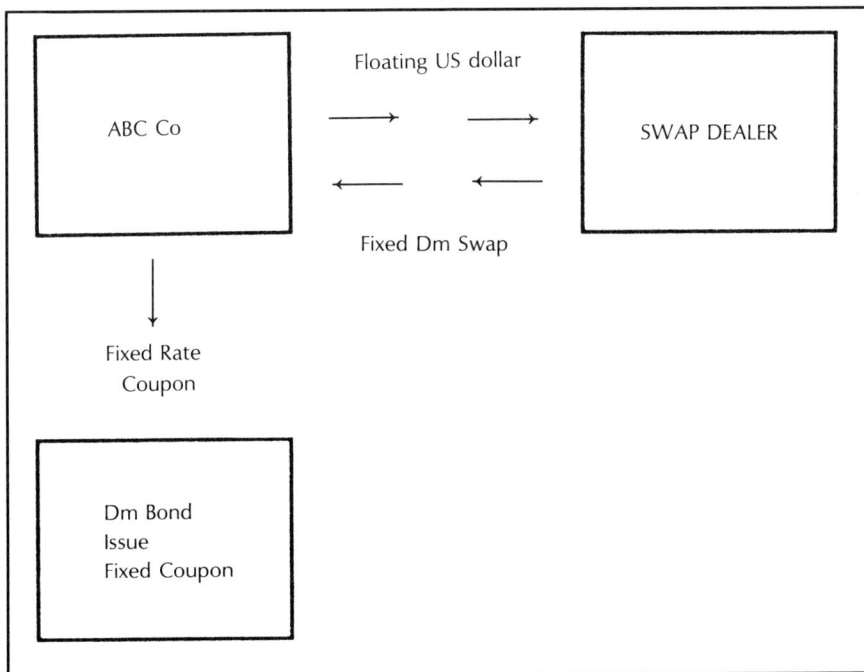

The effect of this is to immunise his underlying liability exposure against a rising Dm and provide access to falling dollar interest rates.

The mechanics of such a transaction are that the borrower, provided the dealing facility is in place, will arrange to swap a principal sum of Dms, in exchange for dollars. Say Dm100 million, in exchange for $50 million (spot rate $/Dm2.00). This may not actually, physically, take place, because the borrowing has already been in existence for some time and probably the bond issue has already been sold for Dms. Therefore one might say that the initial exchange is notional.

During the life of the Swap, interest payments are exchanged, the borrower paying Libor on $50,000,000 (now the income and expenditure can be matched of course). A fixed rate Dm payment is also received, from the Swap dealer, this matches the borrower's Dm liability. At the end of the period of the Swap, an actual exchange of currency, MUST take place and so a payment of Dm100 million will flow from the Swap dealer in return for $50 million from the borrower ABC. The borrower can then repay the Dm bond.

This arrangemen is not dissimilar to a forward contract, or Foreign Exchange (FX) Swap, which involves the selling of one currency for another, with a re-exchange at a later date, when the full interest differential is settled in the FX Swap points. The differences here are that the interest differential is settled periodically, rather than all at maturity and that this transaction is usually much longer than the forward FX market will allow. As such it is likely to be much more price-efficient.

Users

The users of Currency Swaps are the same as the users of Interest Rate Swaps. Credit strength needs to be greater for a given size of deal, because dealing lines (facilities) need to be much larger. The risks in Currency Swaps are very much larger, because whereas in an Interest Rate Swap only interest rate obligations are exchanged, in a Cross Currency Interest Rate Swap, the whole principal sum is exchanged. There is therefore a counterparty exposure to the full sum, often over many years.

Uses

Credit arbitrage allows reduction in funding costs

In the same way that arbitrage in Single Currency Swaps can produce considerable savings, this is also available in Cross Currency Swaps. However, it is less easy to see.

Market access is improved

This gives consequent cost reductions and borrowing in the desired currency, and will include access to subsidised currency export finance packages.

Advantage may be taken of unrealised FX gains

In asset and liability management, a position, which if realised would give a handsome cash profit can be taken advantage of by using a Swap. For example, a borrower has a liability in a weak currency. He would like to lock-in the current exchange rate, but this either means buying the liability currency at today's excellent rate and repaying his borrowing or perhaps covering forward now. First he may not want to repay now, perhaps years early, and he may not be able to anyway. Secondly, the forward market is not generally very liquid beyond six to twelve months.

The answer is to buy the liability currency in the spot market immediately, and simultaneously swap it back for the period of the borrowing. All three exchanges (Spot plus the two ends of the Swap) will be at today's rate, thus the benefit will be locked-in. As in the short-term FX market, the combination of Spot and Swap deal constitute a forward outright position, which given the greater efficiency of the Cross Currency Swap market, will be more competitively priced than an ordinary forward contract for several years.

Yield curve plays

As with single currency plays, maturity transformation is available in cross currencies.

Translation exposure management in assets and liabilities

The problem with exposures of this type is that they are long-term. The usual instruments available in the cash market are thus cumbersome. Options can be used but there is always the question of premium to pay and over many years. Premiums do become expensive when all that is required is some form of fixed-rate hedge. The Swap is therefore more appropriate in maturity profile, and currency gains can be achieved with more subtle use.

In addition, steady cash streams connected with the asset or liability translation being hedged (e.g. profits), which also fall under the heading of translation exposures, can be used to service Swap payments.

Long-term transaction exposures

These may be managed where there is insufficient depth in conventional forward markets.

Portfolio diversification with managed exchange risk

Interest rate arbitrage opportunities, such as those available in the shorter-term FX Swap market, can also be used to enhance yield in longer-term securities.

Structuring the Swap

As with any type of exchange risk management, the key is to examine the currency cashflows involved. The Swap is no exception. Complexity arises out of the need to adjust yields to the desired basis, on top of the structural complications of being involved with two currencies.

The intermediary

The role of the intermediary is to bring two counterparties together, and constructing a deal that is acceptable to both. For this, the intermediary will receive a spread on the deal, in exchange for the risk of one or other of the counterparties failing. (If both fail, no problem, provided no legal loopholes exist to make the situation asymmetric.)

Constructing a Fixed–Fixed Swap

The first type to look at is the Fixed Rate to Fixed Rate Currency Swap and this is best demonstrated.

As an example we will take two counterparties with opposite needs, one a US corporation called Power Cable Inc (PCI(US)) that would like to raise cheap funds in sterling to set up a UK business, but cannot because they are not well known outside the US, and Provincial Airlines Plc (PAP(UK)) a UK airline that would like to borrow dollars to buy aircraft, so that it can service dollar debt from dollar ticket receipts. The problem with such a scheme is that to borrow dollars would not be feasible at the sort of rate that PAP(UK) requires. Both borrowers require fixed-rate funding.

Information: the following rates are available to the parties.

Currency	Term	PCI(US)	PAP(UK)
US$ fixed	5 years	7.00%	8.00%
Sterling fixed	5 years	11.00%	10.50%
Spot £/$1.8000			

Problem

How could we structure a Swap, whereby each accesses the market where they have the greatest comparative advantage, but then swaps into the desired currency?

The first stage is for PCI(US) to borrow $100 m fixed for five years at 7% p.a., leaving PAP(UK) to borrow sterling in London, at 10.50%. The currency amounts will be swapped so creating the desired liabilities.

Step 1

Using the bond calculator, we can calculate how much the dollar debt of PCI(US), ($100 million) will cost each year, at a yield of 7% p.a.

Key	Display
n	5
i	7.00
PV	100,000,000
FV	0
PMT = = = = >	24,389,069.44

We can say that PCI(US)'s debt will amortise over five years at $24,389,069.44 each year.

Thus PCI(US) borrow $100 million and sell this for the sterling it needs at 1.8000 receiving £55,555,555.56 which they invest in their new UK business. PCI(US) will need to receive $24,389,069.44 from PAP(UK) in the Swap.

Step 2

If PAP(UK) are paying $24,389,069.44 to PCI(US), in the Swap, the next question is, how much debt would payments of $24,389,069.44 support at a yield that will appeal to PAP(UK)? Let us suppose that PAP(UK), who we know could only borrow dollars at 8.00% p.a., will be offered financing *via the Swap* at say 7.50%, a saving of 50 basis points. Then by changing the yield in the above sequence to 7.50% and recalculating PV, we find that a payment of $24,389,069.44 will support $98,675,367.82 of debt at a yield of 7.50% p.a.

thus

7.50	i
PV = = = = >	98,675,367.82

At an exchange rate of 1.8000, this is worth £54,819.648.79.

PAP(UK) therefore borrows £54,819,648.79, and exchanges for dollars in the spot market at £/$1.8000. The sterling amount borrowed at a yield of 10.50% p.a., will cost, each year:

n	5
i	10.50
PV	£54,819,648.79
FV	0
PMT = = = = >	14,646,466.82

PAP(UK) therefore borrows £54,819,648.79 and sells this for dollars at 1.8000, receiving $98,675,367.82 and buys their aircraft. They in turn must receive the £14,646,466.82 in the swap from PCI(US).

The account entries so far are as follows:

PCI(US)

Debt

Borrows	$100,000,000.00	(exchanged at 1.80 for £55,555,555.56)

| Pays | $24,389,069.44 | (debt servicing on $100,000,000 at 7%) |

Swap

| Payment | £14,646,466.82 | (Swap payment to PAP(UK)) |
| Receive | $24,389,069.44 | (Swap payment from PAP(UK)) |

PAP(UK)

Debt

| Borrows | $54,819,648.79 | (exchanged at 1.80 for $98,675,367.82) |
| Pays | $14,646,466.82 | (debt servicing on £54,819,648.79 at 10.50%) |

Swap

| Payment | $24,389,069.44 | (Swap payment to PCI(US)) |
| Receive | £14,646,466.82 | (Swap payment from PCI(US)) |

Final step

We know that PCI(US) have exchanged their $100 million debt in the spot market and received £55,555,555.56 for it. They are also paying PAP(UK) £14,646,466.82 each year in the Swap; what yield does this represent?

Key	Display
n	5
PV	55,555,555.56
PMT	−14,646,466.82
FV	0
i = = = = >	9.98% p.a.

Conclusion

From these complex but logical steps, we can deduce the following:

PAP(UK) have borrowed sterling where they are known at 10.50% p.a.
PCI(US) have borrowed dollars where they are known at 7.00% p.a.

They have then swapped into each other's currencies.

PAP(UK) have achieved dollar borrowing at a cost of 7.50% p.a. (Cf 8.00%).
PCI(US) has achieved sterling borrowing at a cost of 9.98% p.a. (Cf 11.00%).

This is illustrated in the following diagram:

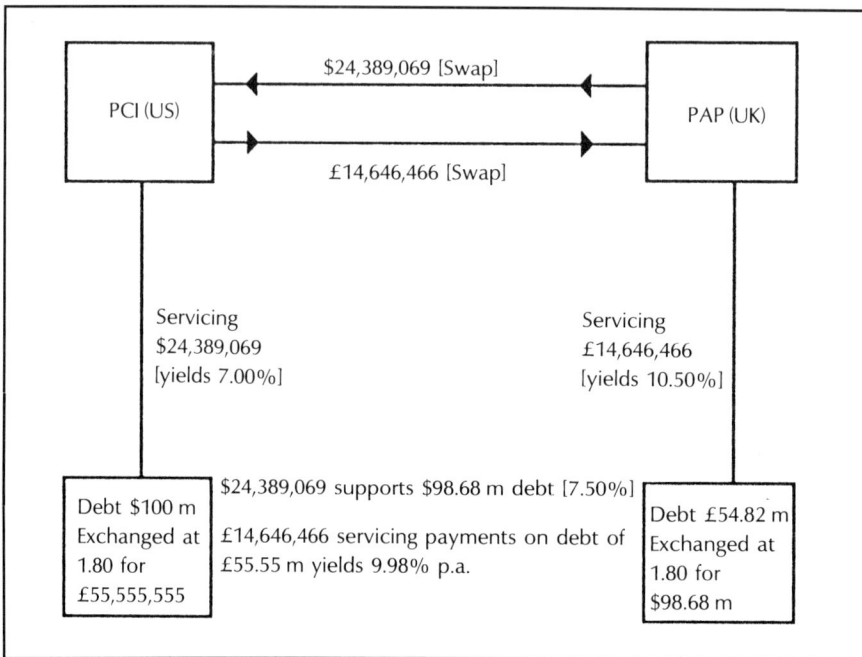

```
┌──────────────────────────────────────────────────────────────────────┐
│                                                                        │
│   ┌──────────┐        $24,389,069 [Swap]        ┌──────────┐          │
│   │          │ ◄───────────────────────────◄    │          │          │
│   │ PCI (US) │                                   │ PAP (UK) │          │
│   │          │ ───────────────────────────►     │          │          │
│   └────┬─────┘       £14,646,466 [Swap]          └────┬─────┘          │
│        │                                              │                │
│        │                                              │                │
│   Servicing                                      Servicing             │
│   $24,389,069                                    £14,646,466           │
│   [yields 7.00%]                                 [yields 10.50%]       │
│        │                                              │                │
│  ┌──────────┐ $24,389,069 supports $98.68 m debt [7.50%] ┌──────────┐ │
│  │Debt $100 m│                                       │Debt £54.82 m│   │
│  │Exchanged at│ £14,646,466 servicing payments on debt of │Exchanged at│ │
│  │1.80 for   │ £55.55 m yields 9.98% p.a.            │1.80 for   │    │
│  │£55,555,555│                                       │$98.68 m   │    │
│  └──────────┘                                        └──────────┘     │
│                                                                        │
└──────────────────────────────────────────────────────────────────────┘
```

Building blocks

An alternative way of creating a Fixed–Fixed Swap is via floating rate dollars. In particular, the Cross Currency Swap market tends to be somewhat illiquid. For example, a fixed rate payer of Deutschmarks direct into fixed rate receiver of yen.

A Swap dealer can create such a Swap out of basic building blocks as follows:

A client requires to pay fixed rate Deutschmarks and receive fixed rate yen, the dealer requires to generate these cashflows through two Swaps:

1. To receive Deutschmarks fixed and pay US dollars floating.
2. To receive US dollars floating and pay yen fixed.

Pricing

Pricing such a Swap is straightforward. Using the prices below, for a five-year deal:

Term	Dm/Dm	yen/yen
5 years	9.18–9.13	7.63–7.60

Hedger pays 9.18 and receives 7.60

This then constitutes two back-to-back fixed floating Cross Currency Swaps.

So far we have not taken into account the necessity to ensure that all prices are quoted on the same terms. The example above illustrates this. Dm/Dm is quoted annual 360/360 (like a Eurobond), whereas the yen/yen is quoted like sterling, act/365, semi-annual. One or other of the quoted yields will therefore have to be adjusted to take this into account.

Details of these adjustments have already been covered elsewhere, but to adjust the yen to the Deutschmark, divide by 365 and multiply by 360 and then compound up to the effective annual rate. Thus 7.60 becomes 7.64% annual 360/360 basis.

14.2 Interest Rate Swaps

An Interest Rate Swap is a contractual arrangement whereby a counter-party paying a rate of interest calculated on one basis can effectively pay a rate of interest calculated on a different basis.

Example

A corporate Treasurer funding his company from a floating rate bank loan (with an interest rate that can change) can effectively turn this into fixed rate (i.e. one that does not change) borrowing, without altering the underlying loan contract, which might cost money. It can be done using a Swap.

The Treasurer may want to do this to avoid rising interest rates.

Cashflow analysis

The best way to understand these instruments is to look at them like Bonds, which are themselves just a series of discrete (periodic) cashflows. A Swap is merely a series of cashflows too.

Essentially what happens in the Swap illustrated above is that the company is offsetting a cash outflow to a lender by importing a similar cash inflow to pay for it, and exporting a third cash outflow which becomes the net cashflow. Thus we can assign pluses and minuses to the cashflows to illustrate direction:

$$-(\text{Cashflow 1}) + (\text{Cashflow 2}) - (\text{Cashflow 3}) = \text{Net} - (\text{Cashflow 3})$$

Cashflows 2 and 3 being the Swap.

Example

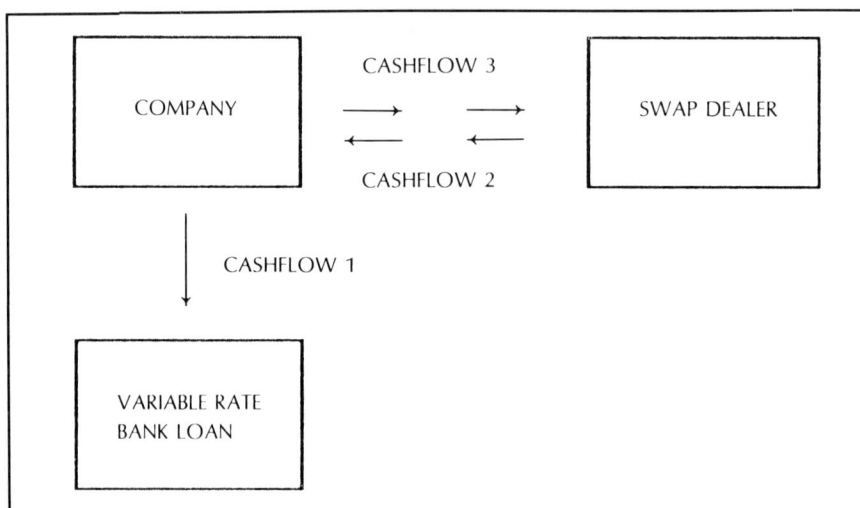

Alternatively

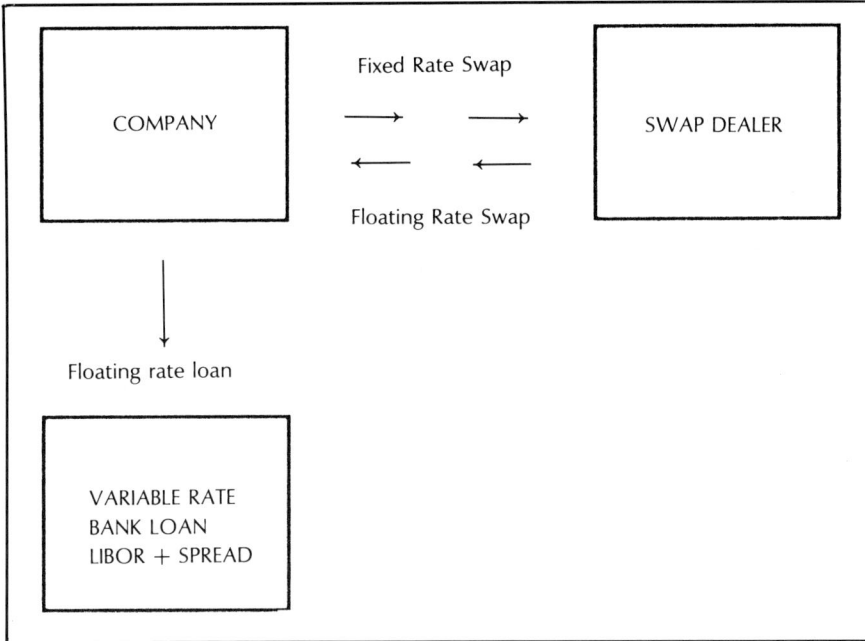

If the two *floating rates* exposures cancel each other out (they may be at different levels but they float together) then the net position is that the company is left with a *fixed rate*, plus or minus any locked-in difference between the floating rates.

In figures this could mean, for example, that a company pays Libor + 25 basis points (on its loan − CF1), receives Libor flat (Swap payment − CF2) and pays fixed rate of 10.04 (Swap payment − CF3).

Net this out, assuming Libor to be 9.50% pa:

−9.75 (interest paid on underlying borrowing)
+9.50 (swap payment 1) ⎱ these being netted out to a
−10.04 (swap payment 2) ⎰ single payment of 0.54%
―――――
−10.29

You have an arranged "synthetic" fixed rate borrowing with an all-in cost (AIC) to the company of 10.29% of the principal amount.

Since Libor is common, we do not really need an actual figure. Merely adding the 25 basis points spread between the two floating rates, to the fixed to reach 10.29% p.a., will be quite sufficient.

Main features

From the illustration you should notice the following:

1. The principal amount is not involved in an Interest Rate Swap, the bank loan remains untouched.
2. The difference between Libor and the fixed rate is netted out to a single cashflow of 0.54% p.a. paid by the company. If later in the life of the Swap, Libor rises above 10.04, then a net payment will flow to the company.

Users

The Swap market is often seen as the preserve of commercial banks who have the credit quality to operate in this environment. Other major players are the supranational organisations like the World Bank, and multinational corporations, once again, who have the credit quality. This is perhaps because these organisations are able to issue fixed rate paper which is very often swapped. Quasi-government organisations like public utilities and export credit organisations are also participants, along with the larger corporates with the sophistication required to operate in this market.

The Swap market should not, however, be regarded as particularly credit conscious; pricing spreads quoted will not necessarily vary because of different credit quality. As long as sufficient credit line is in place when a potential deal is requested, then the deal will be conducted without reference to the credit quality of individual counterparties. That aspect is a matter for those who set up and manage the facility, not the Swap dealer.

Uses

The uses to which Swaps can be put are many and some are extremely complex. They are summarised on the next page.

Interest rate exposure management

- To lock-in fixed rate funding costs, when exposed to floating, when rates are rising or expected to rise.
- Unlocking fixed rate funding when rates are about to fall or falling.
- Unlocking fixed rate investments when rates are rising or expected to.
- To change interest quotation, from one basis (e.g. six-month Libor) to another (e.g. US Prime Rate), to eliminate basis mis-match.

Yield curve plays

- Effectively (but not actually) transforming the maturity profile of assets and liabilities.

Funding

- To create cheaper funding, fixed or floating, through arbitrage.
- To broaden market access.

Structural uses

- To alter balance sheet structure through managing assets and liabilities.

Pricing the Swap

Swaps in themselves are not tremendously complicated in their day-to-day traded form. A considerable market exists in "plain vanilla" fixed floating Interest Rate Swaps which are quoted on-screen, using certain "conventions". The calculations involved in assessing the bottom line cost to the corporate or bank may be made more complex by the necessity to make certain adjustments so that like may be compared with like, again using certain "conventions".

For example, to compare the quoted yield on a Eurobond directly with a US Treasury Bond is incorrect because one pays interest twice a year, the other once a year. This is a matter of differing frequency of payment. There are other differences such as day-year basis, all of which must be taken into account.

Market making

The market maker is the source of all pricing in the Swap market. To come up with the "right" price, any market maker in any instrument needs to be able to construct a theoretical number and then adjust it to meet the market's requirements. For this a benchmark is needed.

Benchmarks

Interest Rate Swaps are normally quoted as a spread over a benchmark government security, in the same way as a commercial bond issue. A Swap may be regarded as creating a kind of synthetic bond.

The bond market is "credit quality-sensitive", however, and works with constant reference to the most convenient credit-risk-free reference point, a government bond in the same currency. UK Gilts for sterling, US Treasury Bonds for US dollars, Bunds for Deutschmarks, JGBs (Japan Government bonds) for yen. Bond issues are then made at whatever price the investor will pay, from which a yield is derived, which represents a spread "over" the government bond. The size of the spread reflecting the quality of the issuer.

The swap is priced at a spread over the government bond as well, but this spread will not vary particularly from one corporate counterparty to another because of differences in credit quality. This can give rise to arbitrage because bond spreads do vary.

Another reason for pricing Swaps out of government bonds, is because where it is not possible to match a Swap, i.e. match two opposing deals on your book, a reasonable hedge can be constructed actually using the appropriate security (referred to as a Hedged Swap). This was more common in the earlier days of the Swap market when liquidity was poor. It is but a logical extension of this to quote "over" the relevant security. There is, of course, no compulsion to match or hedge any Swap, if you wish to run a position.

What do market prices look like?

A look at the Reuters' screen Swap will show a typical view of the Swap market:

	Treasury spreads	USD Swap AMM
2 yrs	T + 97–90	10.93–10.86
3 yrs	T + 85–80	10.72–10.65
4 yrs	T + 72–68	10.54–10.48
5 yrs	T + 72–68	10.49–10.43
7 yrs	T + 72–68	10.39–10.33
10 yrs	T + 72–67	10.33–10.26

The left-hand column shows the maturity of the Swap, a five-year swap commencing immediately and ceasing in five years. It is priced as:

$$T + 72-68$$

What this means is that the *market maker* will receive the fixed (offer side = 72) or pay the fixed (bid side = 68) by adding the spread to the yield of an appropriate US Treasury Bond (USTB), which is usually one with the same maturity as the Swap. The dealer's maximum profit is partly represented by the spread of four basis points, plus a spread on the underlying T-bond as well.

How do we arrive at a price?

The T-bond with five years to run, which we will use to price the Swap, is currently yielding 9.65% p.a. By adding the spread of 0.72% (72 basis points) we can sell a Swap at a rate of 10.37%. You will note, however, that the Swap is actually quoted offered (next column) at 10.49%. The reason for this is that on this particular screen it is quoted on an annualised money market basis (AMMY), whereas the US T-bond is quoted as a semi-annual bond equivalent yield, which has to be adjusted to AMMY.

To complicate things further, many users will often prefer to have the rate quoted as semi-annual money market yield (SAMMY), so even this screen price usually has to be adjusted.

These adjustments to meet certain "conventions" or standard market practices are important particularly when you consider that the customary spread in a Swap is only about four to five basis points. Thus a seemingly minor error in a convention can make a big difference in price – perhaps as much 40 or 50 basis points or 10 times the spread. The correct procedures have already been tried in another chapter on yield comparisons, but we will revisit these important adjustments later.

Buying/selling the Swap, the bid and offer of the market

A Swap is sold to a buyer who pays the offered rate of 72 over USTBs. This actually means that:

The BUYER of a Swap PAYS the FIXED rate.
The SELLER of the Swap RECEIVES the FIXED rate.

One way to remember this is that the buyer of anything from a market maker always pays the higher price; the Swap is no exception.

The market making Swap dealer in the middle thus receives 72 bp (offer) over Treasuries and then pays (the bid of) 68 over, the profit of four basis points in the Swap being retained.

Example

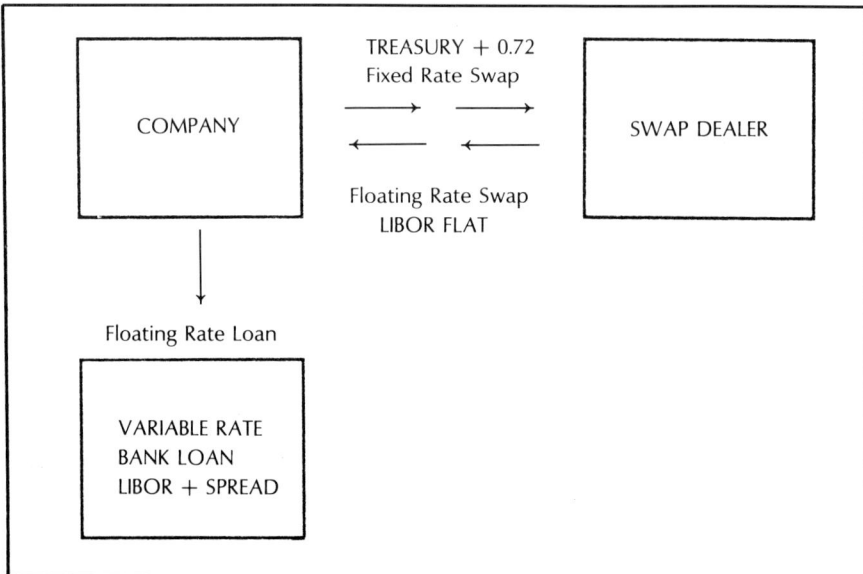

By convention, in a fixed floating Interest Rate Swap, the floating rate payment stream is Libor flat, the spread attaching itself to the fixed payment stream.

Conventions

Having mentioned these several times, it is appropriate to examine the standard practices for quoting Swaps. In reality it is these that cause the complexity and it will put things in perspective if you remember that basically there are only two sorts of adjustment that may need to be made to a price. One is in respect of the frequency of the Swap payment, the other is in respect of the day-year convention.

Returning to our pricing screen displayed earlier, why, if the Swap rate is 9.65 + 0.72 (10.37), (T-bond plus spread) is the rate quoted actually as 10.49 and what does "AMM" mean? This is a so-called "convention", or standard practice in a particular market.

US dollar Swaps like sterling or Deutschmark Swaps all have their own conventions. US dollars are often quoted on an *annualised money market* basis. That is as though the cash flows are paid or received as a *single* payment each year of 365/360 days. (*Actual days/*360.)

However, US Treasury Bonds actually pay interest *twice* a year, on an *actual number of days over the actual number of days*, e.g. 365/365. Thus the USTB + spread will need to be adjusted because it differs from annualised money market basis in two respects; namely frequency and day-year. It makes no difference which adjustment is done first.

First the **day-year** adjustment:

Adjusting 365/365 (US T-bond) or 360/360 (Eurobond) to 365/360 (US and Euro Money Market).

$$\text{Yield} \times 360/365$$

Thus

$$9.65 + 0.72 = 10.37 \qquad adjusted \qquad 10.37 \times 360/365 = 10.23$$

This appears to make the problem worse. What about the 10.49% on the screen, which is now further away than ever from our theoretical price of 10.23%?

Adjusting the convention for frequency will solve the problem.

The US T-bond pays interest *twice* a year in two equal amounts totalling simple interest of (say) 10.37%. Adjusted for money market day-year basis this becomes 10.23%. At this point we have a semi-annual money market basis (SAMMY). This is often adequate for many, but in our case we want an annual money market basis, because that is what is quoted on the screen. This means that we are expecting to pay or receive the fixed side of the Swap less frequently than twice a year, so we will expect to pay (or receive) more to compensate. This therefore involves compounding up the rate.

$$1 + \frac{10.23^2}{200} - 1 \times 100 = 1.05115^2 - 1 \times 100 = 10.49\%$$

A procedure for using the n, i, PV, FV keys follows in the summary, so you will not need to remember the formula. However, to prove that our calculation above is correct, try the following:

Key	Display	
n	2	(always 2 for semi-annual to annual or vice versa)
PV	1	(always 1)
i	5.1150	(10.23/2)
FV = = = = >	1.1049	

The final answer is 10.49 as before (ignore "−" sign).

It is these adjustments which make Swaps more complex than they really are.

In summary

Day-year adjustments

Adjusting 360/360 or 365/365 = = = = > to 365/360 basis
(i.e. you want a lower rate for larger fraction.)

Multiply: **Quoted yield × 360/365**

Adjusting 365/360 = = = = > to 360/360 or 365/365 basis
(i.e. you want a higher rate for smaller time fraction.)

Multiply: **Quoted yield × 365/360**

Frequency adjustments

Adjusting semi-annual (*quarterly*) to annual equivalent
(i.e. less frequent payment demands higher rate.)

> Divide quoted rate by 200 (*400*)
> Add 1
> Square it   (*to power of 4 or square twice*)
> Subtract 1
> Multiply by 100

HP12C procedure

Key	**Display**
n	2 (for semi-annual) 4 (for quarterly annual)
PV	− 1 (invariably)
i	Half of semi-annual yield. Quarter of quarterly annual yield
FV = = = = >	Annual equivalent

Adjusting annual to semi-annual (*quarterly*) equivalent
(i.e. more frequent payment entitled to lower rate.)

> Divide rate by 100
> Add 1
> Square root (*4th root or to power of 0.25*)
> Subtract 1
> Multiply by 200 (*400*)

HP12C procedure

Key	Display
n	2 (for semi-annual) 4 (for quarterly annual)
PV	-1 (invariably)
FV	$1 +$ (Annual rate/100)
i	Half of semi-annual yield. Quarter of quarterly annual yield

Example 10.25% p.a. 360/360
Becomes 10.00% s.a. 360/360
Becomes 9.8630% s.a. 365/360

(This is a 10.25% Eurobond expressed as a semi-annual US Money Market equivalent rate.)

Reminders and hints

When making adjustments you must:

1. Increase price (compound up) for less frequent payment (solve for FV).
2. Decrease price (DE-compound) for more frequent payment (solve for i).
3. Where payment is for a larger time-fraction (365/360) adjust price downwards; when payment is for a smaller time-fraction you adjust price upwards.

Further note

From the Swap screen you will note that Dm Swaps are quoted 30/360 (another variant of 360/360) known as AIBD Basis. For adjustment purposes, this can safely be regarded as the same as 365/365 or actual/actual.

Summary of Swap quotation conventions

US dollar: Annualised money market act/360, (but often quoted semi-annually in actual deals)

Deutschmark: Annual AIBD Basis 360/360

Swiss franc:	Annual AIBD Basis 360/360
Sterling:	Semi-annual actual/365
French franc:	Annual AIBD Basis 360/360
Yen:	Semi-annual actual/365
ECU:	Annual AIBD Basis 360/360

Conclusion

To conclude, the most important thing with conventions is never to assume anything. When you are quoted a price, always make sure of what you are being given. When you are quoting a price yourself, always ensure that your client or counterparty is getting what is required. If in doubt, spend some time on research; it is usually cheaper to solve such problems first!

14.2.1   Swaps — what affects the spread?

The spread between the two sides of the market (bid/offer) are determined by the efficiency of the market and degree of aggression in pricing as in any market using two-way pricing.

The actual absolute level of the spreads themselves over the various government bonds are determined by supply and demand for the fixed payment streams in a Swap. One way of looking at this is to say that if there are many fixed rate issues available for swapping then there is a so-called oversupply of counterparties willing to receive fixed payment streams in the Swap (thus swapping into floating). The spreads they will receive will therefore fall.

On the other hand, a shortage of fixed rate bond issues typically created by an over-supply of liability management Swaps means that receivers of fixed (bond issuers) must be persuaded to receive fixed (therefore pay floating) through the Swap. That incentive is provided by increased Swap spreads. The cost of swapping from fixed liabilities into floating therefore rises.

In other words, if interest rates are rising, there will be increased demand from floating rate borrowers to pay fixed rates of interest through the Swap. This increase in demand will cause the cost of fixed rate funds via a Swap to rise. The government security itself would not necessarily be affected, so the only other component of the Swap price that can move is the spread.

14.2.2 Credit arbitrage

The phenomenon of credit arbitrage is one of the factors which drives the Swap market. This enables the borrower to create low-cost funding opportunities, sub-Libid money etc. By implication it improves market access, by bringing costs down for borrowers who are paying for lack of name or rating in a particular market. So how does it work?

The underlying principle involved is a matter of the differing perceptions of credit risk which exists in different markets. It is a common fact that fixed rate markets discriminate more against weaker credits than floating rate markets. For the economists, it is Ricardo's law of comparative advantage in action.

For example, given a benchmark government bond yielding 10% p.a., an issuer of high quality paper, a sovereign state perhaps, may be able to borrow at 25 basis points over this at 10.25% p.a. in fixed rate markets, with bank lenders charging Libor plus 50 basis points for floating rate funds.

Lesser quality borrowers' paper, if it can be issued in fixed rate markets at all, will have to pay a yield of 12.00% p.a., floating rate paper being at Libor + 100 basis points.

There is thus a demonstrable difference between fixed and floating, between the two types of borrower.

In summary:

Market	Higher quality	Lower quality	Premium
Fixed rate	10.25	12.00	175 bp
Floating rate	Libor + 50 bp	Libor + 100	50 bp

Essentially you can see that the discriminatory premium paid by the lesser quality borrower is greater in the fixed rate markets, by 125 basis points.

Thus, taking the difference between the two, $175 - 50 = 125$, leaves 125 basis points available for arbitrage.

The key to these transactions is to identify the area of greatest comparative advantage. This lies with the higher quality borrower (HQ), in fixed rate markets. (Lower quality is LQ.)

A simple example works like this:

HQ borrows fixed at 10.25:   LQ borrows floating at Libor + 100

Interest rate obligations are exchanged and the arbitrage is split. The LQ pays fixed (12) to HQ, less their share of the arbitrage. This leaves the HQ to pay the floating to LQ.

Swap payments

HQ receives 11.20   *LQ pays 11.20 to HQ*

HQ pays Libor + 100 to LQ   LQ receives Libor + 100

Net position

HQ	LQ
-10.25	$-$ Libor $+ 100$
$+11.20$	-11.20
$-$ Libor $+ 100$	$+$ Libor $+ 100$
$-$ Libor $+ 5$	-11.20
Saves 45 bp	Saves 80 bp

The arbitrage of 125 bp was split in a fairly arbitrary fashion.

A further basic example will illustrate the principle through a Swap priced off the unadjusted US Treasury plus spread.

Five-year Swap, fixed floating US dollars at US Treasuries + 73/70

Market	Higher quality	Lower quality	Premium
Fixed rate	10.25	12.00	175 bp
Floating rate	Libor + 20 bp	Libor + 100	80 bp

HQ borrows fixed at 10.25% p.a.
LQ borrows floating at Libor plus 100 basis points
Swap rate is 10.70/73 against Libor flat

Net position

HQ	LQ
− 10.25	− Libor + 100
+ 10.70	− 10.73
− Libor	+ Libor
− Libor − 45	− 11.73

Saves 65 bp   Saves 27 bp
Dealer spread 3 bp

This time the Libor payment in the Swap is flat, which is more usual.

Note that this does not take into account the various conventions referred to earlier and which must be incorporated into the cost structure.

A further example of a Swap, this time a four-year asset Swap, will take all the conventions into the equation. It is illustrated below.

Four-year asset Swap

The Garrett Fund (London) Plc holds a portfolio of floating rate securities, including some ex-warrant bonds, paying a coupon of Libor + 25 basis points. US interest rates are easing and expected to continue to do so. Libor is currently about 8.50%. The bonds have some four years to run and the US yield curve is positive. The fund managers think that they could usefully transform their asset into a quasi four-year fixed rate issue, by accessing the Swap market. This would effectively lock-out falling short-term yields, creating a dollar Euro-bond-like investment.

Question

What would they achieve in a fixed rate investment? How does this compare with alternative fixed rate Eurobonds?

Term	Treasury + spreads	USD Swap AMM
4 years	T + 72–68	10.54–10.48

Strategy

1. Receive floating on underlying investment.
2. Pay floating in Swap (Libor flat).
3. Receive fixed in Swap (10.48 AMMY).

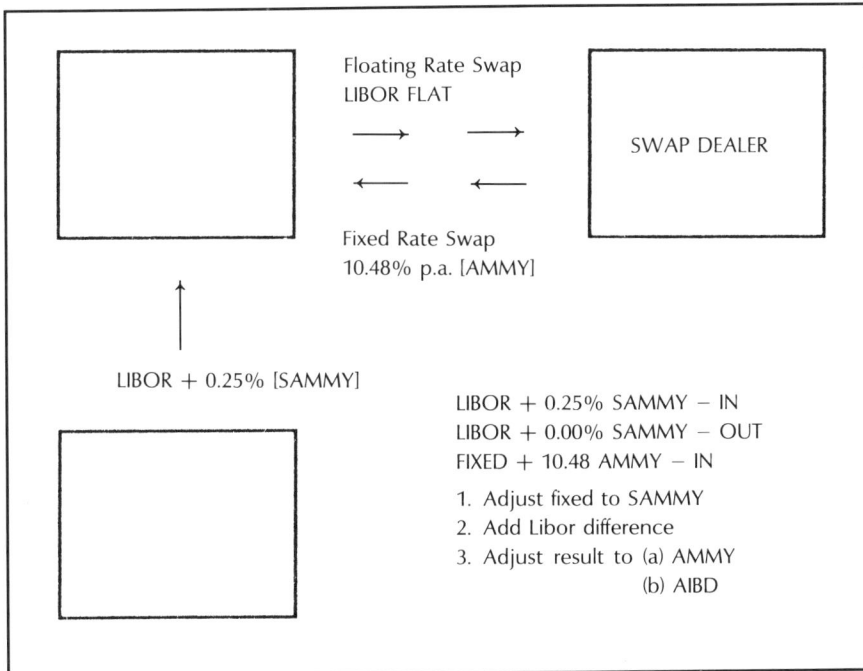

1. Adjust fixed to **SAMMY** by de-compounding (n.b. more frequent flow, lower rate) 10.48 AMMY = 10.2189 SAMMY.
2. Add Libor difference of 0.25 SAMMY = 10.4689.
3. Adjust back to **AMMY** (Eurobonds pay annually) 10.4689 = 10.7429 AMMY.

4. Adjust from 365/360 to 360/360. Smaller time fraction needs higher rate so 10.7429 × 365/360 = 10.8921.

Conclusion

The fund manager has created a synthetic four-year Eurodollar bond yielding 10.89% p.a. Subject to credit risk in asset and credit risk in Swap. Note that the four-year T-bond is yielding 9.92 p.a. on a Eurobond basis.

14.3   Basis Swaps

This sector of the Interest Rate Swap market runs under a number of different titles, namely Basis Swaps, Money Market Swaps, and Index Swaps.

Up to now we have considered only so-called Coupon Swaps, or fixed floating Interest Rate Swaps. Money Market Swaps cater for the bank or corporate user of the Swap market that requires to exchange obligations in say US Prime Rate for Libor, CP for Libor or sometimes T-bill for Libor. More state of the art, perhaps, six-month Libor swapped for six-month Libor reset monthly.

The spreads are quoted as an adjustment to the US Prime, CP or T-bill rate, versus Libor flat. Be careful that the last two are quoted on a yield basis not a discount.

The quotation may look like this:

Term	CP/Libor	T-bill/Libor	Prime/Libor
2	30/34	129/136	− 125/− 122
3	30/33	133/139	− 130/− 125
4	31/36	125/130	− 130/− 125
5	32/37	133/138	− 131/− 125

Example one   CP/Libor

To swap from CP into Libor for two years, a payer of CP at 50 basis points over the composite index will receive CP + 30 and pay Libor flat through the Swap.

Equally, to swap from Libor into CP, a payer of Libor + 30, in a borrowing, will, through the Swap, pay CP + 34 and receive Libor flat.

Example two   US Prime/Libor

Notice that the spreads are negative and the Bid/Offer is reversed. This is because US Prime trades above Libor and the spread remember, is an adjustment to the index other than Libor.

A borrower wishes to swap from being a payer of Prime into being a payer of Libor for five years:

In the Swap pay Libor flat and receive Prime − 131

To swap from being a receiver of Prime into being a receiver of Libor for five years:

In the Swap, pay Prime − 125 and receive Libor flat

The result is such that the receiver of Prime through the Swap receives the maximum deduction from the rate and the payer of Prime through the Swap has as little as possible deducted from it.

A final example brings two together:

A borrower wants to cease paying US Prime and pay CP rate instead, but without a full-blown issuance programme, which will take time and expense to set up. The period required is three years:

Underlying	Pay US Prime
Swap I	Pay CP +33 Receive Libor flat
Swap II	Pay Libor flat Receive US Prime −130

Net result

US Prime	Pays US Prime	
	Receives US Prime less 130 bp	net cost 130 bp
Libor	Libor flat paid and received	net nil
CP rates	Pays (CP + 33)	net cost CP + 33

Merge the cashflows $-(CP + 33) - 130 = -(CP + 163)$ bp

The corporate has simulated CP rates via the Swap at CP plus 163 basis points.

Finally, the Libor 6 to Libor 3 Swap.

Libor Swaps

Supply and demand driven, these Swaps are priced at a spread over the index of up to 12 basis points. In doing so, the compounding effect will be to our advantage if we add it to the shorter index when we receive it and to the longer index when we pay it.

Thus to Swap from paying three-month Libor:

Client will receive Libor three-month
Pay Libor six-month + 10 basis points

In this example we have allowed the client a better spread than the maximum of 12 basis points. Day-year calculations do not enter into the problem as both indexes are money market rates.

14.4   Forward Start Swap

The Forward Start Swap is a formal arrangement to enter into a Swap on a fixed future date, at a prearranged price. Once again the Swap may be constructed from building blocks of individual fixed floating Swaps.

A worked example will show this:

Angstrom B.V. is the Dutch Antilles financing vehicle of a US producer of precision instruments. The company has a future exposure in floating US dollar interest rates, beginning in two years' time and lasting for a period of five years.

How would you price and hedge a fixed floating US dollar Interest Rate Swap, using the following information?

> 2 years 10.61–10.32 AMMY
> 7 years 10.31–10.26 AMMY

Calculate the mean (middle) rate for a two-year and also for a five-year Swap. This will be 10.4650 and 10.2850 AMMY, respectively.

Establish the compounded two-year $(1.104650)^2 = 1.220252$
and seven-year yield $(1.102850)^7 = 1.984336$

Calculate the forward–forward rate from these, two versus seven years.

$$\frac{1.984336}{1.220252} = 1.6262 \text{ (n.b. for five years)}$$

Note that like forward–forward calculations for periods of less than one year (used for the basic pricing of Forward Rate Agreements), the spread is affected if we use the bid and offer rates in the calculation. Therefore we use the middle or mean and spread the resulting forward–forward price.

De-compound this through five years:

Take the 5th root of 1.6262 by inputting

Key	**Display**
1.6262	
ENTER	
5	
1/x	
Yx = = = = >	1.1021 (i.e. to the power of 0.20)

223

Conclusion

The mid-price on an annualised money market yield basis, of a Forward Start Swap beginning in two years and expiring in seven (i.e. lasting for five years) is:

10.21% p.a. versus Libor flat

The counterparty will pay the fixed rate (say 10.23) and receive floating (i.e. hedger buys the Swap).

HP12C procedure

Key	Display
FV	1.6262
PV	-1
n	5
i $= = = = >$	10.21

The trader's position

The Swap dealer can hedge this by entering into a seven-year Swap, paying fixed and receiving floating, simultaneously entering into a two-year Swap, paying floating and receiving fixed. The two Swaps effectively cancel each other out for the first two years, leaving the seven-year Swap with five years to run after two years. The counterparty then pays fixed and receives floating, matching the dealer's cashflows from the established seven-year Swap.

Note on calculation

The routine forward–forward money market formula can be adapted and used to achieve a similar result, but the above method is quicker. As the calculation is a forward–forward by nature, users of the Forward Start Swap can benefit from yield curve effects in much the same way as a money market user of FRAs, Futures and Interest Rate Options.

14.5   Delayed Start Swap

Where the user of a Swap does not wish the transaction to come into effect for perhaps two or three months, then the Delayed Start Swap is more appropriate than the Forward Start Swap.

For theoretical labelling purposes these are technically speaking Hedged Swaps as distinct from Matched Swaps. In other words, the price is quoted based on the cost of the Swap dealer hedging his position in securities and cash, rather than on the prospects of matching one Swap with an opposing one.

If the client wishes to receive fixed and pay floating for example, then the dealer must acquire a fixed and pay a floating payment stream.

The fixed payment stream can be generated by buying the appropriate government security, with a similar or matching maturity. To buy this, the dealer funds his purchase by borrowing in the interbank market at Libor, or at the Repo Rate in the US.

At this stage the dealer has hedged the Swap. It is worth mentioning at this stage that it is not always possible to match the Swap maturity with the appropriate security, because, for example, there may be a scarcity of it, as has happened in the sterling Swap market following the government's reverse auctions in Gilts. In these cases, a security in which there is sufficient liquidity is used and matched to the Swap profile, using such things as Duration.

Outcome

If in say a month the Swap commences for five years and absolute Swap rates have risen, then when the Forward Start Swap commences at the old (lower) rate, the dealer will make a profit from matching the Swap off against current five-year business. However, the yield on the security will have risen in line with the overall Swap rate and the security will be sold at a loss.

More to the point perhaps, if Swap yields have fallen, the Swap dealer will be paying the client fixed at the former (higher) rate and matching against a current five-year Swap at the (current) lower fixed rate, which he will now be receiving. A spread loss will be the result. However, the hedging security can now be sold at a profit (yields having fallen), which represents the adverse change in the present value of the Swap itself. Thus the Swap dealer is hedged.

What is the cost?

Paradoxically it may not be a cost. The cost or gain is basically the difference between the yield on the security purchased (or short sold), and the funding rate (or placement rate), amortised over the life of the Swap.

If, as above, we buy a bond for a month yielding 9.86% and borrow at 13% in the deposit market to do this, we incur a cost of:

$$13.00 - 9.86 \times 31/365 = 27 \text{ bp}$$

For a five-year Swap, amortising this figure over that period adds about 7.50 basis points per annum.

14.6 Amortising Swap

An Amortising structure can be described as one in which the principal amount outstanding over the period of the (usually) loan gets progressively smaller.

The circumstances where an Amortising Swap instrument may be used are to cover interest rate risk on floating rate debt, where the debt itself is repaid in tranches before final maturity. For example, a four-year floating rate note for $100 million, repaid yearly after one year in tranches of $25 million, often referred to as a "sinking fund".

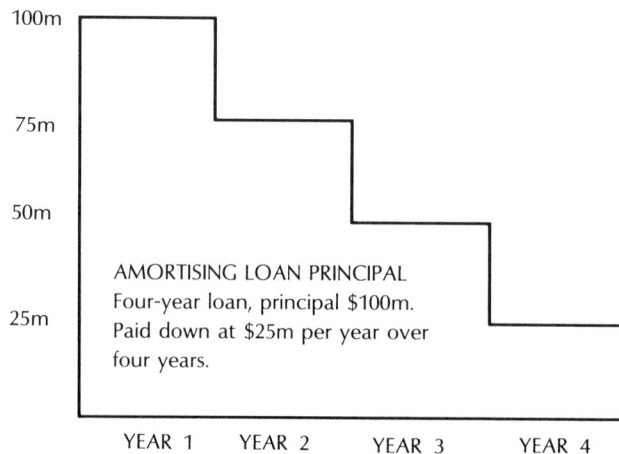

AMORTISING LOAN PRINCIPAL
Four-year loan, principal $100m.
Paid down at $25m per year over four years.

A single fixed floating Interest Rate Swap will clearly not suffice because, after one year, the borrower would be progressively more and more over-hedged. As the differential only in a Swap is paid, this means that a borrower paying fixed and receiving floating, would suffer a substantial cash loss while the fixed rate remained above floating.

The Amortised Swap overcomes the problem. It effectively reduces the value of the Swap in line with the underlying debt being hedged. Pricing may seem complex, but is of a logical "building block" structure.

Assuming the debt described above is being hedged, a number of separate Swap deals must be set up, with amounts to suit the debt profile. Four Swaps will be needed, each starting immediately, but each terminating on a different future date.

1. Four-year Swap for $25 million
2. Three-year Swap for $25 million
3. Two-year Swap for $25 million
4. One-year Swap for $25 million

The profile of the Swap structure is illustrated below.

An Amortising Swap

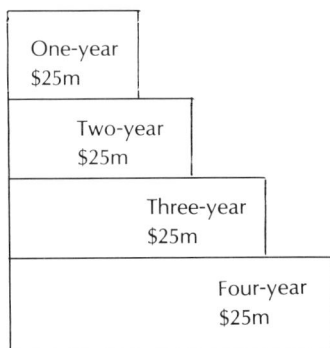

| One-year $25m |
| Two-year $25m |
| Three-year $25m |
| Four-year $25m |

These can now be priced off a screen.

Term	Price	Value	Swap payments
1-year	10.80	25m	2.7000m
2-year	10.60	25m	2.6500m 2.6500m
3-year	10.44	25m	2.6100m 2.6100m 2.6100m
4-year	10.35	25m	2.5875m 2.5875m 2.5875m 2.5875m

Swap payments:	10.5475m 7.8475m 5.1975m 2.5875m

To calculate the overall yield, an IRR calculation will be necessary, which reflects all cashflows (+ = incoming payment, − = outgoing payment).

Principal and Swap payments	Combined total
0. + 100	+ 100 m
1. − 25 − 10.5475	− 35.5475
2. − 25 − 7.8475	− 32.8475
3. − 25 − 5.1975	− 30.1975
4. − 25 − 2.5875	− 27.5875

An IRR calculation using the combined total cashflows, produces a figure of 10.48% p.a.

This can be proved manually by discounting all the cashflows to their present values at the IRR and they will total the principal sum borrowed.

14.7 Swap reversal

Why?

A corporate has entered into a Swap in order to hedge interest rate risk on a floating rate borrowing in view of the greater probability of a rise in interest rates during the early part of the loan. They are paying fixed and receiving floating via the Swap.

After a period of several years, interest rates start to come down and the prospect of being locked-in to a fixed rate, even though this is achieved via the Swap, is unacceptably expensive.

The answer is, within bounds of reasonable cost, to unwind or reverse the Swap, once more effectively paying a floating rate of interest.

Simple reversal

The simplest reversal can amount to a Swap, starting at the next payment date, which opposes the original. The following represents a company that has been paying floating rate in its borrowing and as rates rose, it entered into a five-year Swap, paying fixed at 11.43% p.a. AMMY against six-month Libor.

Now: paying 11.43 p.a. fixed

               receiving Libor

With exactly two years to go, interest rates have peaked and it now seeks to unwind; absolute two years Swap rates are 10.50/10.54 AMMY.

To unwind the original Swap, enter into a new one of two-year maturity, in which the cashflows move in the opposite direction, thus:

               pay Libor

               receive 10.50 p.a. fixed

The Libor payments cancel out. The difference between the two fixed payment streams is:

        11.43 − 10.50 = 93 bp p.a. (AMMY or SAMMY)

Since the company is paying 11.43 and receiving 10.50, the 93 basis points is net cost to them. If this is acceptable to them, then they should proceed. As their floating borrowing rate falls then they will recover the 93 basis points per annum and hopefully more besides in interest rate savings.

An alternative is to terminate the Swap with a single cash payment –
buying your way out of the Swap in this case. It will not always be the
case that there is a loss to cover, however, since a higher fixed rate at
termination in the above example would have provided a cash gain.

Any difference between the fixed Swap rates is easily valued as a single
cash payment, using a bond yield calculator, at current 6m Libor of say
10.00%:

Key	Display
n	4 (number of interest periods remaining)
i	5 (semi-annual simple Libor)
PMT	0.93/2 (locked-in semi-annual cost)
FV	0
PV = = = = >	−1.6489 (present value of all future cashflows)

PV solves in this case as 1.6489. Thus, in a $10,000,000 Swap, we should
require a cash payment of $164,890, immediately, to unwind. This
assumes that all payments due from the last period are made to date and
that the Swap will unwind on the next periodic date which is immediately.

However, life is rather more complicated than this.

Complex reversal

The total cost of reversal now (rather than on a future date) takes a
number of different components into consideration:

The cost/gain of the difference between the agreed fixed rate of the
original Swap and the current fixed rate for the next period, available in
the market, as illustrated above – essentially the cost/gain of a Forward
Start Swap which "counteracts" the original from the next payment
date.

The cost/gain of breaking the current interest payment period. This could be regarded as the present value of the amount yet to accrue, payable on the next payment date under the original Swap.

The present value of the amount already accrued from the last roll-over date, due at the next payment date.

The settlement payment made, whether by the bank or by the counter-party to "buy back the Swap" represents the present value of all these streams.

14.8 Measuring Swap risk

In practice there are three main levels in any market-making institution that are directly concerned with counterparty risk in Swaps.

At the highest level, when dealing Swaps, the dealer is normally only concerned with the existence of sufficient capacity on the counterparty's credit line to allow the successful conclusion of a deal.

At the next level, the client relationship management will take as read the fact that a certain percentage of the principal amount in each Swap must be marked off against his client's dealing line. At this level, the credit analysis is carried out that determines the size of the dealing line or facility.

At the most basic level, the management of the bank must have a clear understanding of the nature of the risk attached to Swaps in order to decide overall risk management policy. This decision governs how much the bank can expose itself to a client in a particular type of transaction and it is pivotal to the other two.

In other words, no amount of assiduous observance of credit limits by the dealer, no amount of care taken by the relationship manager can substitute for understanding the fundamental risks that exist in Swap transactions.

The policy will vary from bank to bank. Typically we might, for example, view the counterparty risk in Swaps as being 3 per cent p.a., with a minimum 3 per cent. Thus a five-year fixed floating Interest Rate

Swap has an overall risk weighting and therefore is marked against dealing lines as some 15 per cent in total. This type of figure may well be fair, empirically, given certain levels of interest-rate volatility. The question is, however, more a matter of the probability of two events happening, than just what can happen to interest rates over time. The 3 per cent p.a. risk weighting assumes that whenever a counterparty fails, rates will always have moved adversely to their historical maximum, which, of course, is highly questionable. Thus, arguments about the impact of off-balance sheet instruments like these will continue.

How does the situation look, using such a parameter as 3 per cent p.a.?

Given a $25 million Swap over five years, then we must allocate 3 per cent p.a. cumulative, in capital, to cover the risk. We can also consider the return on our asset for this degree of risk. This allows us to concentrate, as far as possible, as much of our business as we can in products that have a good risk/reward ratio.

Taking the example, we can develop a table which gives us the information.

The Swap is for $25 million over five years at a spread of 5 basis points.

Years to maturity	Risk for capital	Annual $ income 5 bps	Return on asset	Return required for risk	Profit on asset
1	3% ($0.75 m)	$12.500	167 bp	25 bp	142 bp
2	6% ($1.50 m)	$12.500	83 bp	25 bp	58 bp
3	9% ($2.25 m)	$12.500	56 bp	25 bp	31 bp
4	12% ($3.00 m)	$12.500	42 bp	25 bp	17 bp
5	15% ($3.75 m)	$12.500	33 bp	25 bp	8 bp

Measurement of Swap risk

In general, the risk is measured by considering the cost of replacing a cashflow which no longer exists because of default, by "buying" a replacement equivalent in the market at current rates. The arithmetic is the same as for Swap reversals. At any time the value of a Swap can be calculated by marking to market. This in itself illustrates the folly of using a blanket percentage per annum limit for marking Swaps off against a dealing line, since we could easily find that the counterparty is exposed to the market maker and not vice versa. Thus risk is two-sided.

The following example will show how we mark a Swap to market and thus evaluate at any time what risk we are running.

Marking to market

A bank entered into a seven-year Swap two years ago, and has been receiving a fixed sum of 10.26% in exchange for paying floating Libor flat. In order to mark to market we assume the worst. With five years to go, a default by the counterparty who has gone into liquidation would mean that this fixed rate cash payment stream has to be replaced at current market rates.

There is also a smaller risk that if default occurred between reset dates, there could also be a Libor difference.

In summary, in order to evaluate our position we should examine what it would cost (or pay us) to find a replacement. We would need to receive fixed and pay floating rate for five years. The loss (or profit) we stand to make will be governed by where absolute Swap rates are now.

If perhaps they are at 9.26 per cent, then we stand to lose 1 per cent p.a. (i.e. $10.26 - 9.26$) for the next five years. We have replaced a 10.26 per cent fixed income stream with a 9.26 per cent p.a. income stream.

All that remains to do here is to analyse what our cash loss would be now. If Libor is say 13% then our loss is 3.52% of the principal amount. This is actually the present value of five lost payments of 1 per cent each year, discounted at today's Libor yield, 13.00%.

The calculations on an HP12C render the whole thing much simpler.

Key	Display
n	5 (number of years we would have to carry a loss)
i	13 (discount rate for PV calculation)
PMT	1 (amount of each year's loss difference)
FV	0 (loss amortised to zero in five years)
PV = = = = >	−3.52 (current present value)

In other words, this is rather like saying that if we set aside 3.52 per cent of the notional value of the Swap in capital now, and invested this at 13 per cent, then we would have enough to meet our obligations to the other counterparty.

Swap risk in Cross Currency Swaps

This is far greater than Single Currency Interest Rate Swaps. All that has been said already about Swap risk applies to Cross Currency Interest Rate Swaps, but *in addition*, there is a substantial exchange risk.

The risk is the same as forward contract risk, which is of the order of 20 per cent for a year and 10 per cent per annum beyond that. The greater risk arises because, as we have seen, principal may have been exchanged but *must* be re-exchanged. There is, therefore, always the danger of the unmatched outright currency position, if default occurs.

If a counterparty, for example, exchanges $100 million dollars, receiving sterling in return, at the inception of a five-year Swap, it is on the assumption that the US dollars will be returned and the pounds given back after five years have elapsed.

If, after four years there is no prospect of the dollars being returned because of default, then they must be purchased in the cash market at the going rate and the pounds sold. What could that rate be after four years, given recent levels of currency volatility? Certainly it could be very different. Over the last five years, sterling has been as low as US$1.0350 and as high as almost US$2.0000. The potential for loss is therefore huge.

234

It is this and the resultant risk weighting that is applied for capital adequacy purposes that has meant that the Cross Currency Swap takes a relatively smaller role compared with Single Currency Interest Rate Swaps.

A specific example might look like this.

Bank A Swaps US$100,000,000 with company C, receiving Dm150,000,000, at the inception of a five-year Swap, at 8.00% fixed in Dm against floating dollars. In five years' time they will expect to receive $100,000,000 back, and pay Dm150,000,000. This is based on an exchange rate of 1.5000.

After two years, company C fails. At that time Swap rates have changed by 1 per cent and the value of the losses when the Swap is marked to market are calculated in exactly the same way as above, 1 per cent p.a., for three years, discounted to Present Value. On top of this, however, the exchange rate has changed and the dollar has strengthened – it is now worth 1.9500.

In order to replace the $100,000,000 owed in the Swap, they will cost Dm195,000,000, or the Dm150,000,000 they have will only buy $76,923,076.92. This is a loss of over 23 per cent plus the interest rate risk.

IV Mathematics for FX markets

15   Forward FX hedging using money market transactions

An exposure is basically made up of two components:

a) Time
b) Currency position

In order to immunise the effects of exchange rate movements on a currency asset or liability position, this involves the covering of an exposed position by, first of all, dealing at spot. This takes care of the currency position.

For example, a sterling-based organisation with a Deutschmark receivable due in six months' time, may be represented graphically as follows:

Spot (T2)   Forward (T180)
                                    + Dm (exposure)

Sell Dm @ 2.8325   (A spot deal executed
Buy UK£   at current market rate)

Having dealt at spot selling Deutschmarks to the market and buying sterling in return at 2.8325 the rate is fixed. The residual problem is solely one of time. The foreign currency is not due for six months.

The solution is to borrow the foreign currency and invest the resultant sterling amount, until the currency receivable arrives. The objective is to cover the risk, not generate a sterling cashflow at spot.

The picture will now look like this:

```
T2                              T180
                                + Dm
-----------------------------------------------------------------
    + Dm (borrow at 6.00)     − Dm (repaid)
    − Dm (sold at 2.8325)
    + UK£
    − UK£ (invest at 11.00)   + UK£
-----------------------------------------------------------------
```

From the foregoing example it can be seen that to carry this transaction through, assuming the interest rates are fixed, will result in the company apparently earning 5 per cent p.a. in interest, over and above the spot rate. It should be noted that this is simplified for illustrative purposes.

The reverse situation

If the situation was reversed, i.e. a Deutschmark payable was involved, then the borrowing/investing would also be reversed and there would be a forward cost involved.

This cost would not be the same as the forward earning, there being other factors to be taken into account. In a transaction of this kind, the borrowing may be subject to a margin (1 per cent p.a. in the example). In addition, the base lending rate, and the investment rate, will be subject to the normal bid/offer money market spread.

Other costs/earnings considerations

In addition there are other possible costs/earnings to choose from. Borrowing in this context can be a very loose term that includes the use of working capital, or unutilised balances being used instead of formal borrowing. Alternatively, rather than invest the proceeds of a spot deal, working capital could be created instead, the relevant true return on the funds then being more a question of the return on capital.

More advanced use of such systems involve bringing future deals forward as outlined above, to avoid predicted adverse changes in exchange rates, and holding receivables to benefit from improving exchange rates. These activities are, of course, speculative.

Hedge evaluation

Accurate evaluation of the hedge is a little more complex than taking just the interest differential. At this stage, it will suffice to say that the method of calculating the accurate cost or gain of achieving the forward position employs the following process:

1. Identify the currency of the exposure, the *target* currency.
2. Calculate the gross interest differential between the two currencies.
3. Discount this differential at the target currency interest rate, for the number of days that the position is held.

Example

    Yen 7.80–7.92%

    Dollar 8.87–9.00%

    Dollar/yen 150.00

To buy yen forward, using the money market hedge, will cost:

Borrow US$	9.00%	
Buy yen	at	
Sell dollars	spot	Cost differential 1.20%
Invest yen	7.80%/	

Differential discounted at yen interest rate for a year:

$$\frac{1.20}{1.0780}$$

$$= 1.11\% \text{ cost p.a.}$$

If the period is less than one year, the annualised differential should be discounted for the period involved.

16 Forward pricing and Swap pricing up to one year

The creation of a hedge using the basic money market technique can often be expensive for the smaller company, ties up working capital and uses up credit lines. It also fills up the balance sheet which may be undesirable. Using a six-month Deutschmark exposure, illustrated in an earlier section, an alternative hedge might be the Forward Exchange Contract, as an off-the-shelf product.

The cashflows for an exposure hedged in this way, will look like this:

```
T2                          T180
                            + Dm      (receivable)
-----------------------------------------------------------------
                            − Dm      (sell currency)
                            + UK£     (buy currency)
```

This represents the sale of a Deutschmark receivable in six months' time at a rate agreed today.

How does the dealer arrive at such a rate?

The basis of the pricing is the simple money market hedge-structure. In the forward exchange contract, the client has passed its Deutschmark position (a long position) to the dealer, at the 180-day point. The bank's exposure is thus identical to the client's original exposure. Using the money market transaction, the bank borrows Deutschmarks and sells them, buying sterling at spot off the market, for investment, until ultimate delivery to the client.

Example: bank exposure to client

T2	T180
	+ Dm(from client)
	− UK£ (to client)

- -

+ Dm(Euro offer rate)	− Dm (repaid to Euromarket)

− Dm (sells Deutschmarks to the spot market)
+UK£ (buys sterling from the spot market)

− UK£ (Euro bid rate)	+ UK£ (repaid by market)

- -

The next stage is to plug in some market rates for the various deals done:

Spot £/Dm	2.8330/60
Euromarks	6 m 5.125–5.00% p.a.
Eurosterling	6 m 11.125–11.00% p.a.

From the example we can deduce that a forward earning will accrue to the bank, of $11.00 - 5.125 = 5.875\%$ p.a. and this will be passed on to the client. The spot rate concerned will be 2.8360, the market selling price of sterling.

Such an arrangement rarely exists in real life. It is, nevertheless, valid as a pricing model for forward exchange rates. For instance, a dealer does not of course give the client the spot rate and pay interest (or charge it for a transaction in the opposite direction), on the amount concerned; instead, the spot rate is adjusted to take account of the forward earning, or in the reverse situation, the forward cost. The basic forward rate is therefore a calculated rate, not some view of where the spot rate will be in the future. Position taking, market forces etc., will then move the rate away from this theoretical base, until arbitrage brings it back thus imposing a limit to the amount of movement away from the theoretical price.

The spot rate is adjusted by using the forward points, Swap points or forward margin according to well established basic rules of adding discount points (quoted low on the left, high on the right) as against subtracting premium points which are quoted high on the left side, low on the right.

Using our simple pricing model, we can calculate a forward margin by calculating the implied forward rate and establishing the difference between that and the spot rate. This leaves us with the forward points or margin or Swap rate. This mechanism is usually referred to as the square (see below).

A simple example first, creating about 3000 + Deutschmarks

     UK£/Dm 3.0000

     UK£ 1 year 10%

     Dm 1 year 5%

Borrow £1000   Repay £1100

Sell £1000
Buy Dm 3000

Invest Dm 3000   Recover Dm 3150

Implied forward rate (i.e. the cost or value of £1.00) is 3150/1100 = 2.86361 representing a margin of 0.1364. Notice that this is not 5 per cent of 3.0000 (0.1500) as one might expect.

The following formula will produce the same result.

$$\frac{\dfrac{\text{Spot} \times (\text{interest differential}) \times \text{days}}{3600}}{1 + \dfrac{(\text{interest*} \times \text{days})}{100 \quad 360}}$$

*Important: the interest rate in the lower part of the formula must be that of the base or reference currency, the unit of one in an exchange rate.

244

We can now substitute rates used earlier for a six-month deal:

Spot £/Dm 2.8330/60
Euromarks 6 m 5.125–5.00% p.a.
Eurosterling 6 m 11.125–11.00% p.a.

Substituting

$$\frac{\dfrac{2.8360 \times (11.00-5.125) \times 180}{36000}}{1 + \dfrac{(11.00 \times 180)}{36000}}$$

$$= \frac{0.0833}{1.0550}$$

$$= 0.0790$$

Thus the outright forward rate for buying Deutschmarks from the client in 180 days is:

$$\begin{array}{r} 2.8360 \\ \text{minus } 0.0790 \\ \hline = 2.7570 \end{array}$$

The client therefore gives up less Deutschmarks to the bank in 180 days than he does at spot. The forward earning from the interest rate differential is so incorporated into the rate.

Looking at a transaction where the dealer is selling the currency to the client, there would be a forward cost arising out of the money market structure (i.e. borrow sterling and invest Deutschmarks) and therefore the amount of Deutschmarks paid must be adjusted downwards.

Substituting the rates again, but from the opposite side of the price:

$$\frac{\dfrac{2.8330 \times (11.125 - 5.00) \times 180}{36000}}{1 + \dfrac{(11.125 \times 180)}{36000}}$$

$$= \frac{0.0868}{1.0556}$$

$$= 0.0822$$

This results in an outright forward price of 2.7508 to pay Deutschmarks to the client in six months.

Summary: spot £/Dm   2.8330/60
           6 m points   822/790

Note on formula: the interest rate in the lower half of the formula will always be the interest rate of the reference currency, in this case sterling. Sterling is the unit of one in the quotation method used (Dm 2.8330 = £1.00) and therefore the amount must be matched in the forward calculation.

With other exchange rates such as dollar/Deutschmark, US dollar is the reference currency.

16.1   Evaluating costs and gains in Forwards and Swaps

The currency hedger has a bewildering array of instruments and techniques at his disposal. Hedging by borrowings, investment of currency, paying early for a cash discount (i.e. leading) delaying payment because it is a cheaper source of funding than borrowing elsewhere, using currency options, collars, all of which conventionally have their costs and/or earnings expressed wholly or partially as a percentage which may be annualised quite simply.

246

The exceptions to this are Forward Exchange Contracts and FX Swaps. Both have their costs/earnings expressed as points, added to, or subtracted from, the spot rate.

When considering the choice of instrument or technique for hedging, it is necessary to compare the annualised costs/earnings of each. This is only possible where they are all expressed in the same terms, i.e. as annualised percentages.

The following formula (a simplified reverse of the forward points formula) will achieve this:

$$\frac{\text{forward points}}{\text{spot/forward outright}} \times 360 \times 100$$

Remembering that the lower figure in a set of points is always the hedger's forward earning (i.e. the dealer always pays the smaller points), the higher the forward cost (i.e. the dealer always charges the higher points).

We can then calculate the annualised percentage (gain) in the following example.

A US exporter is making a shipment of electronic components to Germany. These are worth about US$50,000 and are shipped on 90 days' credit. At the time, current spot and forward dollar/Deutschmark rates are quoted as follows:

Spot	1 month (30)	3 month (91)
$/Dm 1.7980/90	54/51	175/170

From this information we can see that the relevant spot rate is 1.7990 with 1.7820 as the (better) three months outright rate, including 170 points premium. The exporter has a choice as to which one he uses, depending on the forecast scenario. To help in the decision, a figure which can be compared with other hedging media and rate forecasts will be useful. The formula allows a percentage figure to be employed.

$$\frac{0.0170}{1.7820} \times \frac{360}{91} \times \frac{100}{1}$$

$$= 3.7740\% \text{ p.a.}$$

In this example, it can be seen that to cover a forward receivable in Deutschmarks in the forward foreign exchange market for a period of three months the hedger earns some 3.77 per cent p.a. He might consider offering a discount incentive, based on this figure.

The technique can also be used to make comparative hedging decisions, as mentioned in an earlier paragraph, using borrowing, options, leading for a cash discount, etc., all of which have their benefits or penalties expressed as some form of a percentage gain or cost.

Two versions of the formula

Earlier in this handbook you will perhaps have noticed that the basic formula we used allowed for either the spot rate or the outright forward rate to be used.

$$\frac{\text{Forward points}}{\text{Spot/forward outright}} \times 360 \times 100$$

In the example above, we used points over the forward rate; this is usual for all sterling-based organisations with exposures expressed in the foreign currency. It is also appropriate for US dollar-based corporations with exposures expressed in foreign currencies, *except those involving sterling*. Under certain circumstances, we must use the spot rate; the latter is one of them.

The use of the alternative formula depends on which way the exchange rate is quoted. For example, rates quoted against the US dollar are normally quoted as the number of units of foreign currency per one dollar. An exception to this rule is sterling, which is quoted inversely, as the number of US dollars per pound sterling.

The effect of changing the method of quotation can be demonstrated, using the dollar/Deutschmark exchange rate, normally quoted as Deutschmarks per dollar, but often quoted as cents (dollars) per Deutschmark, for instance on Futures Exchanges.

	Spot	One year	Points
Normal quotation	1.8155	1.7655	0.0500 [−]
Inverse quotation	0.55081245	0.56641178	0.01559933 [+]

Points as a percentage of spot

Normal quotation (NQ)	2.75%
Inverse quotation (IQ)	2.83%

Points as a percentage of Forward Outright

NQ	2.83%
IQ	2.75%

The conclusion that can be drawn from this is that points/spot normal quotation equals points/forward inverse quotation.

Where is this likely to cause a problem?

If a borrower is trying to decide the cost of funding in a foreign currency and covering the exchange risk using the Swap, the cost/earnings of the Swap will need to be analysed, to decide which of a range of foreign currencies is the cheapest, or if the cost of funding in base currency is the lowest after all. The all-in-cost of funding in this way is the sum total of the interest rate on the currency and the Swap.

To compare the bottom line the borrower must ensure that the exchange rates are quoted the same way. A US organisation in determining the cost of funding in sterling or Deutschmarks will be involved with exchange rates quoted differently, i.e. dollar/Deutschmark and sterling/dollar. Either rate could be inverted, but this moves away from standard global FX practice. Instead, the formula is modified.

There is an easy rule of thumb that can be used to make sure that comparisons really are comparable. Note that base currency in this context means home currency.

Take the *normal* method of quotation (e.g. $/Dm).

If the base currency of the hedger is *first* (i.e. US dollars) then use points over *forward* rate. (Note: obligation expressed in Dm.)

If the base currency of the hedger is *second* (i.e. Deutschmarks) then use points over *spot* rate. (Note: obligation expressed in dollars.)

This would indicate that the percentage cost/earnings of a forward deal for a US base is different from those of a German base. This is actually true, because they start from different reference points. An example will illustrate this.

We will use only one price for each date for clarity.

Rates: spot 1.8155   year 1.7655

German based	Exposure in one year
	− US$1,000,000.00 (payable)
Spot value	Forward value
Dm 1,815,500	Dm 1,765,500 2.75% earning (spot)

Using the correct version of the formula:

$$\frac{0.0500}{1.8155} \times 100 = 2.75\% \text{ p.a.}$$

If we look at an identical value exposure, but from the other point of view:

US based	Exposure in one year
	− Dm 1,765,500 (payable)
Spot value	Forward value
US$972,459.38	US$1,000,000.00 2.83% cost (spot)

Using the correct version of the formula:

$$\frac{0.0500}{1.7655} \times 100 = 2.83\% \text{ p.a.}$$

The German hedger has a 1 million dollar exposure, the US hedger has a million dollar equivalent in Deutschmarks at the forward rate. This demonstrates that how the obligation is quoted affects the use of the cost/earnings formula.

Summary

Assume Normal Quotation

Base currency first	use points over	Forward
Base currency second	use points over	Spot

17 Long-dated forward rates

Introduction

Long-dated forward contracts are very similar in their nature to the ordinary forward contract, available in a wide range of currencies, in the forward exchange market. As a means of hedging against adverse exchange rate movements, they have their place. Generally speaking, however, the long-term Swap market is likely to be more efficient and therefore more cost-effective.

A forward contract is a binding contract to exchange specific amounts of currencies at a predetermined rate of exchange, for delivery on a future date. In the short-term market, simple interest rate differentials are used to calculate the rate. In the long-dated market, over one year, compound interest rate differentials should be used.

Using the following information we can construct a rate for a five-year forward deal, exchanging dollars for pounds.

> Spot £/US$ 1.9200
>
> £ five-year rate 12% p.a.
>
> $ five-year rate 9% p.a.

Using compound interest theory, the five-year accumulated value at each rate of interest is:

$$1.12^5 = 1.762342$$
$$1.09^5 = 1.538624$$

Dividing the base into the quoted currency, as we do in an ordinary forward contract, and multiplying the ratio by the spot rate, gives us the outright forward rate.

$$\frac{1.538624}{1.762342} \times 1.9200 = 1.6763$$

Thus a five-year forward exchange could be conducted at 1.6763, a difference of 0.2437 under the spot rate.

Broken dates can be calculated using fractional indices.

18   Covered interest rate arbitrage and yield enhancement

Arbitrage opportunity

The forward foreign exchange market relies principally on the interest rate differentials in the Eurocurrency market, for its pricing. In the section covering the pricing of forward contracts and FX Swaps, we saw that taking two interest rates, one for borrowing, the other investing and coupling them to the spot rate through a formula provides us with a theoretical price. Given the supply/demand forces in the market place moving prices away from their theoretical basis; given the technical inefficiency of the market producing a certain amount of price disparity between institutions and other factors such as overheads, an available Swap price may very well be theoretically out of line with an available interest differential. Such discrepancies, provided they are large enough to pay dealing costs and overheads, will open up profitable arbitrage opportunities. The opportunities are rarer these days and disappear more quickly, because the market is more efficient. Nevertheless, opportunities do appear but they disappear more quickly.

Funding and investor opportunities

In reality opportunities manifest themselves in the ability to create base currency monies cheaper via a Swap, than direct from a base currency cash market. They also give rise to the phenomenon of yield pick-up on securities, such as Commercial Paper, involving creating a "synthetic" security, not available in the cash market at the calculated yield. This section concentrates on yield enhancement in short-term securities. In practice, whether opportunities exist or not for arbitrage, the same evaluation calculations are used to "bottom line" any scheme involving a switch into and out of a second currency.

254

The mechanics

An investor with US dollars to place, requiring liquidity and security has the obvious choice of investing in US Treasury Bills, if a short maturity, liquid, safe, security is required. By using the foreign exchange market, more specifically the forward FX market, he also has an ability to invest in London, in UK Treasury Bills, protect himself against exchange rate fluctuations and enhance yield, all at the same time.

A worked example should demonstrate this, but note that we are seeing the transaction from the investor's point of view, so purchases of currency must be made at the going rate out of the market. Sterling is bought at the market-offered rate and sold at the market-bid rate. If you are a dealer, making markets, arbitrage should not rely on the availability of a convenient client to whom you can make a price.

Market information

> Spot £/$ ... 1.5980–90
>
> 91-day Swap ... 0.0273–0.0270

UK T-bills yield 15.45% on 365/365 basis (15.2383% USMM basis).

From this we can work out what sort of yield we can expect by Swapping into sterling and investing in a 91-day UK T-bill.

1. Buy and sell £10,000,000 Spot against three months, paying 273 points in the Swap. Note that the Swap will be a mismatched deal, to cover the yield earned on the T-bill.

+£10,000,000	Principal	−£10,000,000
−$15,990,000		+$15,717,000
	Interest	−£385,191.78 (91 days at 15.45%)
		+$605,405.92
1.5990		1.5990
		273
		1.5717

Total dollar cashflows

Paid $15,990,000   Received $16,322,405.92

. . . . . Growth $332,405.92 . . . . .

$$\text{Yield:} \frac{332,405.92}{15,990,000.00} \times \frac{360}{91} \times 100$$

$$= 8.22\% \text{ p.a. (USMM)}$$

This represents an annualised yield of 8.22%. At the time of writing 91-day US T-bills yield 8.03%. A yield pick-up of some 19 basis points.

This calculation can be carried out in a less cumbersome way using an arbitrage equation:

$$I^d = I^{nd} -/+ (\text{gain/cost of Swap}) -/+ (\text{gain/cost of forward cover on } I^{nd})$$

where

I^d = domestic currency rate of yield (in this case US dollars)

I^{nd} = foreign currency rate of yield (in this case sterling)

Note that this example involves a US-based investor, whose domestic currency is US dollars and to whom sterling is the foreign currency.

A general inclusive formula will look like this:

$$I^d = I^{nd} -/+ \left[\frac{\text{Swap rate}}{\text{Spot/fwd}} \times \frac{360}{\text{days}} \times 100 \right] -/+ \left[\frac{\text{Swap rate}}{\text{Spot/fwd}} \times I^{nd} \right]$$

Note that if you are starting from the base currency as your domestic currency e.g. $ in $/Dm or £ in £/$ or Dm in Dm/yen and moving into the other currency, then the formula version includes:

$$\frac{\text{points}}{\text{forward rate}}$$

If you start with the non-base currency, as your domestic currency, e.g. Dm in $/Dm, $ in £/$ or yen in Dm/yen, then use the formula version involving:

$$\frac{\text{points}}{\text{Spot rate}}$$

Substituting in the equation (the domestic currency is dollars in this case), I^d is what we are trying to calculate, and we use Swap rate divided by spot.

$$I^d = 15.2383 - \left[\frac{0.0273}{1.5990} \times \frac{360}{91} \times 100 \right] - \left[\frac{0.0273}{1.5990} \times 15.2383 \right]$$

$$= 8.22\% \text{ p.a. (USMM)}$$

Where I^{nd} is the foreign currency you are investing in and I^d is the currency you presently hold. Arbitrage will tend to drive the equation into equilibrium, in that it should not theoretically be possible to create one currency from another via a Swap at a different yield than the original currency, but market inefficiency and individual position-taking will cause price discrepancies to occur which will allow occasional "windows" to occur.

Additional worked example

This example starts with a UK investor organisation (domestic currency therefore pounds sterling) seeking a yield pick up by swapping into US dollars and investing in Euro CP. The advantages for the investor will be an enhanced yield, through the Swap arbitrage, broader market access and investment and the exchange risk is covered automatically by the Swap.

Information

Value date of transaction	12 December '90
Issue date of paper	27 November '90
Maturity date of paper	12 March '91
Original maturity	105
Days left to maturity	90
US Euro day-year	Act/360 (i.e. USMM)

Sterling day-year	Act/365 (i.e. UKMM)
Coupon of paper	8.69% p.a.
Current yield maturity	8.42% p.a.
Current Spot £/$ rate	1.5805
Current 90-day Swap rate	0.0247

The objective is to "manufacture" a sterling yield out of a Eurodollar yield together with the Swap.

Mechanics

Buy US dollars to purchase paper at current price and sell forward face value via the Swap, earning 247 points in the process, which may be added to the dollar yield on the paper.

Effective domestic yield on Act/360 basis:

$$8.42 + \left[\frac{0.0247}{1.5558} \times \frac{360}{90} \times 100 \right] + \left[\frac{0.0247}{1.5558} \times 8.42 \right]$$

$$8.42 + 6.35 + 0.13$$
$$= 14.90 \text{ (Act/360 basis)}$$

Adjust to Act/365 $14.90 \times 365/360 = 15.11\%$ p.a.

Conclusion

The synthesised sterling yield from the entire transaction is 15.11%, which may then be directly compared with similar investment media.

Notes

Because we start from a sterling base, and move into dollars, we should use the version of the formula where the Swap rate is divided by the forward rate.

The FX market uses a day-year basis of Act/360. It is therefore important to adjust the final sterling yield to Act/365, in compliance with normal UK money market convention.

19 The calculation of currency volatility

In foreign exchange markets the talk is often of currency volatility, the big unknown that affects all managers of currency risk, by the uncertainty that it introduces into the management of such risk. In option writing, it is volatility that is the one "unobservable" pricing component. One might say that for an identical option, priced at the same time by two different writers, any difference in quoted premium is largely accounted for by the writers' assessment of future volatility, all other variables being the same.

The variable inserted in all the pricing models has to be a matter of judgement based on a mix of numbers obtained from three sources:

> Historic volatility
>
> Implied volatility
>
> Forecast volatility

It is the calculation of historic volatility which we cover here, which can then be used as a trader thinks fit. The arithmetic of the various models used in pricing options is not under consideration here, because there is much software available commercially which does this. An analysis of the arithmetic of these models would serve no useful purpose; however, a working knowledge of the calculation of the oft-quoted volatility numbers will lead to a better understanding of these important statistics.

The calculation of historic volatility

General

Certain assumptions have to be made about volatility; these assumptions are dangerous unless tempered. The assumption that past volatility will be the same in future is unwise and might be compared with driving one's car in a forward direction using only the rear view mirror. Nevertheless, an idea of "where we have been" is necessary, and indeed is a basic tenet of technical analysis, so first we calculate historic volatility. The calculation is purely a statistical analysis, of rate fluctuations, during a sufficiently long period, say daily, for a year.

Stage one

Assess what rate movements have taken place for the period. On a bar chart, this will give large numbers of small movements and smaller numbers of large movements, all centred about a mean or average.

The calculation of annualised percentage historic volatility

Given an accumulation of data, we can calculate our historic volatility. The figure is quoted as a percentage, usually annualised.

The example that follows cannot be particularly representative because the sample of rates is very small, one a week, which would not be nearly enough under the circumstances. Nevertheless it will demonstrate the principles involved. Normally, data would be collected on an almost continuous basis. The discrete nature of the worked example is untypical in that respect.

The various columns below represent the stages in calculating what is known as the standard deviation of percentage rate changes. Standard deviation (if you like, the amount of fluctuation), is a measure of volatility. If you wanted a definition of a currency volatility number it could be described as one annualised standard deviation of the percentage changes in historic exchange rate movements.

Using dollar/Deutschmark, the following tables rate changes that took place over a ten-week period at weekly intervals.

	Col 1	Col 2	Col 3	Col 4	Col 5
1	1.8000	—	—	—	—
2	1.7920	−0080	−0.0045	−0.004190	0.00001756
3	1.8100	+0180	+0.0100	+0.010310	0.00010630
4	1.8265	+0165	+0.0091	+0.009410	0.00008855
5	1.8385	+0120	+0.0065	+0.006810	0.00004638
6	1.8525	+0140	+0.0076	+0.007910	0.00006257
7	1.8150	−0375	−0.0205	−0.020190	0.00040764
8	1.7890	−0260	−0.0144	−0.014090	0.00019853
9	1.7720	−0170	−0.0095	−0.009190	0.00008446
10	1.7950	+0230	+0.0129	+0.013210	0.00017450

Overall % Change =   −0.0028*   0.00118647

$$\text{Mean of the \% change } (+/-) = \frac{0.0028}{9} = -0.00031$$

*The mean is a negative indicating that the peak of the normal distribution is below zero. This in turn indicates that movements downwards have been larger than upward movements, hence the final rate in the sample (1.7950) must be below the first rate in the sample (1.8000).

What it actually says is that "on average" rates have moved down by 0.03% (0.0003) each week. This does not help you very much because it does not tell you what has happened in between.

Using conventional statistical arithmetic, the standard deviation is the square root of the sum of the squares (total of column 5), divided by the number in the sample (9 changes plotted) less 1.

$$\text{Standard deviation} = \sqrt{\frac{0.00118647}{9-1}} = 0.01217826$$

Notes

Column 1: Exchange rates
Column 2: Absolute changes in rates

Column 3: The degree of change here is calculated by taking the natural logarithm of the ratio of the rate change. It is very similar to percentage change, as a decimal

$$\frac{\text{Rate } 2}{\text{Rate } 1} \text{ LN} \quad \text{e.g.} \quad \frac{1.7920}{1.8000} \text{ LN} = 0.0045$$

Column 4: Deviation from mean = i.e. 0.00031 − Column 3
Column 5: Deviation squared (removes pluses and minuses in data)

Since the above data were taken weekly, over a ten-week period, it follows that the standard deviation of percentage weekly rate changes is:

$$0.01217826$$

For an annualised standard deviation figure you must multiply this by the square root of 52.

$$7.21 \times 0.01217826 = 0.08780525$$

By convention, we say that volatility is *one standard deviation, in per cent, per year*. Our conclusion, from the weekly data above, is that annualised volatility is 0.08780525 or *8.78 per cent per annum*.

What does this actually mean?
The whole point of the analysis is to enable certain forecasting assumptions to be made, for hedging purposes.

If the current rate of exchange for $/Dm is 1.5000 now, and volatility is quoted as 10%, what will it be in a year's time?

We cannot predict absolute exchange rate levels by using the volatility number.

What we can do is say the following, given the information above.

We expect the rate to trade between:
$$1.3500 \text{ to } 1.5000 \text{ to } 1.6500$$
for 2/3 of the time

We can therefore say what our maximum and minimum losses and profits are likely to be, given the current levels of volatility of 10 per cent. This allows us to hedge our position rather more scientifically.

V   Mathematics of short futures contracts and FRAs

20　Forward–forward interest rates

A forward–forward rate is that rate that will apply to a loan or deposit beginning on a future date and maturing on a second future date.

Example

A corporate borrower enters into a contract which will fix the rate of interest that will apply to a loan beginning in six months and repayable after a further six months. In other words he has entered into a forward–forward interest rate contract, six months against twelve months, often called sixes/twelves.

In order to understand the pricing of such a contract which fixes the forward–forward interest rate, we need to examine the way in which a corporate could achieve a forward–forward rate using deposit trading techniques.

Forward–forward loan:　　　1. Borrow NOW
　　　　　　　　　　　　　　2. Invest until funds needed

Forward–forward deposit:　　1. Invest NOW
　　　　　　　　　　　　　　2. Fund by borrowing

The drawbacks to this method are several:

1. Uses up credit lines immediately on deposit and loan transactions.
2. The locked-in rate will be more expensive because of margins.
3. Roll-overs are difficult to cover.
4. Unwinding could be expensive.
5. Inflates the balance sheet. (This may or may not be disadvantageous.)

The alternative is to ask a bank to carry out the transaction instead, using its own credit lines immediately and avoiding the effect of margins on the calculated forward–forward rate. This is, however, comparatively rare, but the concept of a forward–forward rate is still nevertheless important, because it forms the foundation for the pricing of Interest Rate Futures and Forward Rate Agreements, the over-the-counter futures transaction.

Market interest rates: US dollar Libor

> three-month 5.81–5.93
>
> six-month 5.81–5.93

N.B. A flat yield curve for the period in question. This does not mean that the threes/sixes forward–forward rate will also be 5.81–5.93.

Pricing procedure

1. Bank borrows $1,000,000 from the market at 5.93% p.a. for six months fixed, paying interest at the end of the period of $29,650.
2. Funds reinvested back in the market for three months at 5.81% p.a. earning $14,525.
3. Net costs are therefore (29,650 − 14,525) or $15,125 and this sum must be recovered over the final three months when the bank lends to the customer, if the bank is not to lose money.
4. You will note that the bank does not have to pay interest until six months have elapsed. It receives an interest payment, however, after three months. This mismatch in interest payments has the effect of reducing funding costs. In other words, the bank has the interest after three months as a contribution towards its funding costs.

The break-even point then may be assessed by calculating the net costs as an annualised percentage of principal plus total earnings.

$$\frac{\text{net costs}}{\text{principal} + \text{earnings}} \times \frac{360 \times 100}{\text{days in period}}$$

Substituting

$$\frac{15,125.00}{1,014,525} \times \frac{360}{90} \times 100$$

$$= 5.96\% \text{ p.a.}$$

The same principle can be used to calculate the forward–forward deposit rate, using the appropriate rates, by depositing long in the market and borrowing short.

The outcome can be calculated by taking net earnings as an annualised percentage of principal plus total costs. On this occasion it should be borne in mind that the interest mismatch (bank pays out on the three-month borrowing before it receives interest on the six-month deposit) works against it and produces a lower forward–forward rate because of the additional funding of the three-month interest.

The whole question can be simplified by using a ready-made formula, one of several different versions that achieve the same result.

$$\frac{1}{T2 - T1} \times \left(\frac{(T2 \times R2) - (T1 \times R1)}{1 + \left(\frac{(T1 \times R1)}{36000} \right)} \right)$$

where
  T1 = short period in days
  T2 = long period in days
  R1 = short period interest rate
  R2 = long period interest rate

The formula should be applied using the following rates. .

Forward–forward deposit

  Use R1 at market offered rate

  Use R2 at market bid rate

i.e. borrow short and lend long off the market.

Forward–forward loan

  Use R1 at market bid rate

  Use R2 at market offered rate

i.e. borrow long and lend short off the market.

From previous example of $1,000,000 forward–forward loan rate:

$$\frac{1}{180 - 90} \times \left(\frac{(5.93 \times 180) - (5.81 \times 90)}{1 + \left(\dfrac{(5.81 \times 90)}{36000} \right)} \right)$$

$$= 5.96\% \text{ p.a.}$$

Where sterling is involved, the basis of Actual/365 should be used, at other times use Actual/360.

Forward–forward interest rates as we have seen are obtained by calculation and are the rates that will apply to future deposit or loan periods. The forward–forward is rather more important as a pricing mechanism for Interest Rate Futures, Forward Rate Agreements, Interest Rate Options, and Forward Start Swaps, than as a hedging device in its own right.

It is also useful in running a money dealer's book, in that the formula can be used to work out arbitrage against futures and FRAs, against natural, mismatched positions in the book.

The bid–offer spread

When you calculate a forward–forward rate in the manner we have just used, you will realise that the bid–offer spread is magnified greatly. As a result, when calculating future rates from interest rates, a middle rate is normally used.

21 Time deposit futures pricing

Introduction

For completeness, this section examines the arithmetic of futures pricing. As noted in the introduction, it does not aim to give a comprehensive guide to what futures are and how they are used in hedging and trading, since there is a wealth of publications which already cover the subject.

Following the section covering forward–forward interest rates, the pricing mechanism of time deposit futures is quite straightforward; in fact it uses the same forward–forward formula and we will not repeat this here. In case of difficulty, you should refer back to the previous section.

The way the price is quoted in the market is a little strange to the uninitiated, but it is logical.

21.1 The quotation of the price in the market.

All time deposit futures, whether on the IMM in Chicago or the LIFFE market in London, are quoted in the same way, that is:

$$\text{Price} = 10 - \text{the forward–forward yield}$$

For example if the forward–forward yield is 6 per cent per annum then the price of the contract will be $100 - 6.00 = 94.00$, usually just quoted as 9400.

The contracts are traded as three-month time deposits, linked to Libor, in US dollars, sterling and Euromarks, beginning in March, June, September and December.

Why is the price quoted in this way?
The nature of the contract means that, say in November, the buyer of

269

one December contract acquires a contractual obligation to deposit $1,000,000 and receive a rate of interest determined by the purchase price. Note that the contract will not actually be delivered, but a compulsory cash settlement is made, which amounts to the same thing. Thus using the numbers above, the buyer of one lot of the December contract at 9400, is obliged (in a manner of speaking) to place a million US dollars, on deposit, at a rate of interest of 6% per annum, for a three-month period, beginning in December and ending in March. The 6 per cent is thus a forward–forward rate, set in November, to apply to a transaction beginning in a month.

Let us suppose that interest rates fall. In December if the deposit rate for US dollars in cash is less than 6 per cent our contract buyer will be in a better position. The price of the contract rises to reflect this, e.g. $100 - 5.50\% = 9450$.

In summary, the price of the contract moves in the opposite direction to the rate of yield, like a fixed-interest security.

21.2   The hedging principle

The hedging arithmetic in time deposit futures necessitates the calculation of two things, first the profit (or loss) in the futures position and secondly the loss (or profit) in the hedged cash position.

As with all hedging in futures, the basic principle is that a hedge is constructed in a parallel but leveraged market, the futures market. The object is to make sufficient profit out of a position in futures to cover any deterioration in the cash position. If, however, the cash position moves in the hedger's favour, this will cause a loss on the futures position. The overall effect is therefore to eliminate upside potential as well as eliminating the downside element. Hedging by running a contract to expiry and then taking delivery is extremely rare.

* * *

Contract: ED3 $1,000,000 (a three month time deposit)

Maturity dates available: March, June, September, and December

Initial margin:	US$1000 per contract (this changes from time to time)
Variation margin:	US$25.00 per tick of one basis point

Delivery on the third Wednesday of the month of delivery, last trading day being two days prior.

Price quotation 100 − annualised forward–forward yield

***

The use of the ED3 (three-month Eurodollar) contract for hedging purposes can be demonstrated in the following example.

Genco Marinas S.A. plan to build a marina in the Mediterranean and this will be partly financed by Libor-based bank borrowing.

The loan will be for US$3,000,000 drawn all at once at the beginning of June, on a six-month Libor basis. Current rates are 6 per cent p.a. with the corresponding forward–forward rate for June being 6.10 per cent, the yield curve sloping upwards and steepening indicating that markets think that rates will rise during the period being hedged.

The hedging strategy will take the following form, illustrated below, with the interest rate exposure itself on the left and the futures position on the right.

Cash market	**Futures position**
1st January:	
Future borrowing US$3,000,000 in five months on 6m Libor.	Sell six ED3 contracts for June price 100 − 6.10 = 9390. Margin of $6000 paid out.

Interest rates rise

1st June:	
US$3,000,000 drawn down and rate (6m Libor) rises to 7.00% p.a. Half-year costs rise to a	Buy futures (six ED3 contracts price 100–7.10 = 9290). Margin payments paid in 100 ticks, a

new amount US$106,166.67
(182 days).

gain of 100 × US$25.00 per tick
per contract = 2500 × 6 giving
a futures profit of US$15,000.00.
Initial margins repaid in full.

Net interest paid 106,667.67 − 15,000 = 91.667.67

further $$\frac{91,667.67}{3,000,000.00} \times \frac{360}{182} \times 100$$

$$= 6.04\% \text{ p.a.}$$

Summary

By taking an appropriate position in futures, the hedger has made as much profit from the movement of rates as he has lost from that same rate movement, which cost him $15,166.67 in increased borrowing costs.

21.3   The calculation of variation margin

The US$25.00 per basis point, or tick as it is called, is worked out as follows:

The contract unit size is US$1,000,000.00 and this changes in value by US$100 per annum, for every basis point change in interest rates. Since the contract is a *three-month* time deposit, divide the US$100 by four and you arrive at US$25 variation margin.

21.4   The hedge ratio

You will note that the number of contracts we used was six, even though the value of the exposure was only $3,000,000.00, or three times the value of the contract unit size. This is because the exposed position was a *six-month* time deposit, whereas the contract standard is a three-month time deposit.

The formula for working out the correct ratio of contracts to use is:

$$\frac{\text{value of exposure} \times \text{length of coupon period in days}}{\text{contract size} \times 90}$$

Applying the figures used earlier:

$$\frac{3,000,000.00 \times 182}{1,000,000 \times 90}$$

$$= 6.06$$

We should therefore use six contracts in the hedge.

Which contract we use is a matter of judgement. A conventional hedge would perhaps involve using the contract which expires just beyond the maturity of the exposure. Alternatives will involve splitting the six used in the hedge so that during the six-month borrowing, three expire as drawdown takes place and three more half way through. Other strategies may involve the selling of the futures contract which has adequate liquidity and is trading at a high price.

22 The Forward Rate Agreement

The Forward Rate Agreement (FRA) is a contract between two parties that determines the rate of interest that will apply to a future loan or a deposit which may or may not materialise, an agreed amount of an agreed currency to be drawn or placed on an agreed future date for a specified term.

The FRA is quite a simple instrument, in that it offers to compensate the party that stands to lose by an interest rate movement, by means of a cash payment, from the party that stands to gain. There are two sides to any FRA transaction.

How does it work?

The basic idea is one of mutual compensation for adverse movements in interest rates. The party that stands to gain compensates the party that stands to lose. It is very much like a futures trade in this respect, but with no margin calls.

22.1 Terminology

The FRA will cover the notional loan/deposit period called the **contract period**, in a **contract amount** of the **contract currency**.

The contract period begins on the **settlement day**, when the cash compensation is paid. The end of the contract period is called the **maturity date**. In order to know how much compensation to pay, an **agreed**, **guaranteed** or **future rate** is applied (actually the "price" of the FRA). This will be what determines the rate that will apply to the notional contract amount. The future rate is then compared with an agreed reference point in the market, the **reference rate** (often page 3750 Telerate), on **fixing date**, and the difference between the agreed future

274

rate, and the reference rate is paid in cash, calculated using the formula below. Fixing date and settlement date are the same for domestic currency, fixing date being two days earlier in foreign currencies.

The borrower buys an FRA to protect against a rise in rates, the depositor or lender sells an FRA, protecting against a fall.

Compensation formula

$$\frac{CA \times (F - L) \times CP}{360 \times 100} \times \frac{1}{1 + \left(\dfrac{L}{100} \times \dfrac{CP}{360} \right)}$$

Key:

CA = Contract Amount   (notional loan/deposit amount)
  F = Future Rate (guaranteed
       rate)   (the quoted price of the FRA)
  L = Libor Reference   (market interest rate on fixing
                   date)
CP = Contract Period   (length of interest periods)

    (F − L) may be reversed (L − F) to avoid negative numbers

Note that the compensation payment is made (whether the customer or the provider is paying) at the beginning of the notional loan/deposit period, thus it is discounted to its present value.

22.2   Pricing

The FRA is quoted as a two-way price, with a bid and offer as with deposit rates.

The prices themselves are derived from interest rate futures. A formula you will have enountered in forward–forward interest rates is repeated below; the futures price is derived from this.

The FRA price is always Libor based. This does not have any significance for the depositor, since the reference rate is also a Libor rate and the rates are therefore comparable and move the same way.

1. Six-month Eurodollar 8.37 (183 days)
2. Twelve-month Eurodollar 8.50 (365 days)

Formula

$$\frac{(LP \times LR) - (SP \times SR)}{1 + \dfrac{(SR \times SP)}{(360(5) \times 100)}} \times \frac{1}{LP - SP}$$

LP = Long period, SP = Short period
LR = Rate for long period, SR = Rate for short period

Substituting

$$\frac{(365 \times 8.5) - (183 \times 8.37)}{1 + \dfrac{(183 \times 8.37)}{(360) \times 100}} \times \frac{1}{365 - 183}$$

$$\frac{1570.79}{1.042548} \times \frac{1}{182} = 8.2785\% \text{ p.a.}$$

This is the implied yield of the futures price of 9172 (100 − 8.28). The 6m/12m FRA would then be quoted at about 8.25–8.30.

22.3 Hedging arithmetic using FRAs

A corporate borrower seeks interest-rate protection for a six-month period beginning in six months' time. (A 6m v 12m forward–forward position.) Amount of the proposed borrowing will be US$5,000,000 and forecasts are for an increase in rates over the period of the loan which is on a three-month Libor basis.

Requirements

Two FRAs priced as follows:

	Dealer 1	Dealer 2
1. 6m v 9m	6.21–6.15	6.23–6.18
2. 9m v 12m	6.28–6.22	6.30–6.25

Buy at 6.21 and at 6.28 from Dealer 1, both prices being cheaper. The simplest evaluation for a "strip" hedge, such as this, is to calculate the average rate for the six-month contract which is 6.25% p.a. It should be noted that the more accurate way of calculating the cost of funds for the period is through an internal rate of return calculation.

If interest rates do move up to perhaps 7% then using the compensation formula, the borrower will receive the following cash payment on settlement day:

$$\frac{5,000,000 \times (7 - 6.21) \times 91}{360 \quad \times \quad 100} \times \frac{1}{1 + \left(\dfrac{(91 \times 7)}{360 \times 100} \right)}$$

$$= US\$9,811.12$$

If rates then continue up to 7.375% p.a. at the first roll-over then the compensation payable to the borrower will amount to US$13,586.30 (using the FRA rate of 6.28%).

The overall effect is to produce an average borrowing rate of 6.25% which is clearly better than the market. Futures can be compared with this, but the costs of margining should be taken into account.

22.4 Odd period pricing and broken dates

This section covers the techniques which are used to price FRAs for parameters which do not coincide with the futures market. In the strict sense, one might not consider an FRA that covers something as standard as six-month Libor to be odd. However, there is nothing available in the futures markets anywhere, that corresponds to a six-month contract period. Therefore it has to be worked out from the futures prices available in the three-month.

Sample prices, in November; implied forward yields in parentheses:

December   9400   (6.00)

March	9380	(6.20)
June	9365	(6.35)
September	9340	(6.60)

How do we calculate an FRA, with a contract period from December to June, i.e. a one-month versus seven-month FRA.

1. Take the quarterly flat yield of the December (three-month) contract at 6.00%.
2. Take the quarterly flat yield of the March (three-month) contract at 6.20%.
3. Compound the two together, to a six-month nominal rate.

$$1 \qquad\qquad 1 + \frac{6.00}{400} = 1.0150$$

$$2 \qquad\qquad 1 + \frac{6.20}{400} = 1.0155$$

$$3 \qquad\qquad (1.0150 \times 1.0155) = 1.030733$$

$$3.07033 \times 2 = 6.1465\% \text{ p.a. (the six-month nominal rate)}$$

We have used basic compound interest arithmetic to produce a six-month rate which corresponds in yield to the effective yield of the two three-month "strips". This is the price of our ones/sevens FRA.

What happens if we cannot precisely match the futures dates?

Then we need to calculate the correct FRA price off the futures, either side of the date we want, and pro-rata between the two.

22.5 Broken date FRA pricing

We have calculated the FRA price for a contract period starting in December and ending in June. A 1/7 FRA. How do we arrive at a reasonable price for an FRA that starts later than December, but earlier than March, and similarly has a contract period of six months?

Repeating the futures prices:

December	9400	(6.00)
March	9380	(6.20)
June	9365	(6.35)
September	9340	(6.60)

We know the December to June FRA is 6.1465% from earlier calculations. We now need the price of the March to September FRA, which is:

1
$$1 + \frac{6.20}{400} = 1.015500$$

2
$$1 + \frac{6.35}{400} = 1.015875$$

3
$$= 1.031621$$

$3.1621 \times 2 = 6.3242$ p.a. (the six-month nominal rate)

We now have two six-month FRAs overlapping:

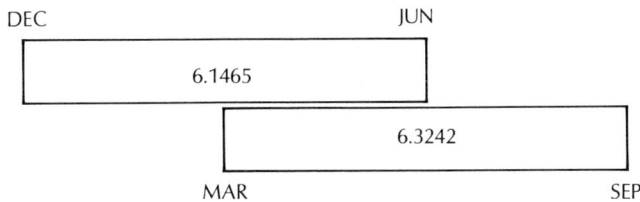

In concept, if we need an FRA for a six-month contract period beginning between December and March, we can either slide the Dec/Jun towards the Mar/Sep or the other way round. For every day that we slide the upper block over the lower block we must adjust the rate.

The difference between the FRAs is 6.3242–6.1465 or about 18 basis points. With perhaps 90 days between December and March fixed dates, this is 0.20 basis points per day.

Therefore if we want an FRA that begins 15 days after the December 1/7, then we quote $6.1465 + (15 \times 0.20) = 6.1765$. or 6.18.

23 Using IRR to evaluate strip hedging

Strip hedging is the technique of using instruments such as Futures and Forward Rate Agreements in sequence, one following another.

For example, if a corporate treasurer wanted to borrow money for a year, starting immediately, he might consider borrowing in a number of different ways, to meet his objective of arriving at the lowest funding cost. We will consider two possibilities, although there would be more.

If the currency being borrowed has a negative money market yield curve, consideration should be given to whether borrowing at the 12-months' fixed rate is a lower rate than the current three-month cash rate and a strip of three FRAs. You will recall that when we covered FRAs a flat yield curve produces a lower FRA rate. An inverted yield curve exaggerates this effect quite dramatically.

How do we evaluate the total yield on a year's projected borrowing using three months cash and a strip of three FRAs following?

Cash 3 months	13.00%
3/6 FRA	12.58%
6/9 FRA	12.00%
9/12 FRA	11.50%

Conventionally, we can assume that the FRA price will be the cost of borrowing, excluding any margin. It is this basic cost that we are concerned about. What is the annual nominal rate off these figures? First, an average would be a useful indicator; this is 12.27%, but this is not necessarily accurate. For example, does the fact that we have a high rate to start with increase the cost? An average ignores this. Internal Rate of Return does not.

For IRR, we will need the quarterly flat figures, these are:

13.00/4 = 3.25
12.58/4 = 3.145
12.00/4 = 3.00
11.50/4 = 2.875

We use these figures, but in conjunction with a principal as well. You will recall that all formulae involved in yield calculations must involve a principal put in at the beginning and removed at the end. The IRR procedure is no different.

Now, using the techniques learned earlier for IRR, input the data, including a notional principal sum, at the beginning and at the end.

Key

− 100	g CFo
3.25	gCFj
3.145	gCFj
3.00	gCFj
102.875	gCFj
f IRR = = = = >	3.0723

Multiply by four for the annual nominal rate and you have 12.29% p.a. Compound up for the annual effective rate. It is the latter at 12.8672 that you should look at to compare with the 12-month fixed rate.

Notes on keystrokes

Remember the CHS key to change the signs for the cashflows; this is vital.

Conclusion

The figure of 12.29 is an accurate representation of the cost. The average of 12.27 is too low, because it does not take into account the fact that the interest cost is higher in the earlier months.

To evaluate against the costs of borrowing one-year fixed, compound at the quarterly IRR of 3.0723.

Key	Display
i	3.0723
PV	-1
4	n
FV $= = = = >$	1.1287

We can read off the effective rate for the quarterly roll-over of 12.87%. If the 12-month rate is lower, serious consideration should be given to borrowing in the longer maturity, provided interest is payable annually.

VI The arithmetic of equities and linked instruments

24 The arithmetic of equities

The investor in ordinary shares, equities or common stocks seeks the best return on the original investment and will compare different stocks to achieve the optimum balance of risk and return. This chapter seeks to explain how the various ways of assessing yield are calculated.

The arithmetic used to calculate yields and values is similar to bond maths, because the returns on common stocks (like most bonds excepting zeros), are a matter of income and the change in capital value.

For comparison purposes, a table is published in the *Financial Times* which sets out averages and indices of the various measures we will consider, for each industrial and business sector. It is against these that the performance and yield of a given share can be compared and any differences accounted for and explained.

24.1 Dividend yield

The first ratio used in yield assessment, and therefore company performance, is to calculate what the dividend paid by the stock is in terms of its price. This is dividend yield.

For example, a 50 pence share in ABC Petroleum Plc pays a dividend of 22 pence and its quoted price is 296 pence. The current dividend yield in this case is:

$$\frac{\text{Dividend} \times 100}{\text{Price}}$$

Substituting

$$\frac{22 \times 100}{296}$$

$$= 7.43\%$$

The dividend yield of this share is 7.43% and such a number may then be compared with shares in companies in the same market sector, with comparable risk ratings. It is usually calculated gross, rather than net of tax.

This number only accounts for the amount of earnings paid out in dividend. It takes no account of the amount of the earnings reinvested in the company, nor of the growth in the share price during the period in which the dividend was earned. It is simply a measure of the amount of income obtained from the investment in the original share price.

24.2   Earnings per share

Perhaps a more meaningful measure of performance, because it takes into account the total earnings of the company, is the EPS ratio.

This is made up of:

$$\frac{\text{Profit after tax}}{\text{Number of ordinary shares issued}}$$

Using the earlier example:

A 50 pence share in ABC Petroleum Plc pays a dividend of 22 pence and its quoted price is 296 pence. The current dividend yield is 7.43%.

Profit for the year, after tax, was £1,800,000 and the number of shares issued is 7,000,000.

Thus:

$$\frac{1,800,000}{7,000,000}$$

$$= 25.71 \text{ pence}$$

Earnings per share works out at 25.71 pence. This takes account of the total earnings and not just those paid out to shareholders in the form of dividend. When compared with dividend, an investor can see how much earnings has been distributed and how much retained in the company for future use. With an oil company this might be important if its proven oil reserves are low and it will need to embark on an exploration programme.

24.3   Price/earnings ratio

The third common ratio used to assess performance in a stock is the P/E ratio. This is calculated by using the earnings per share figure (and thus takes into account the total earnings after tax) which is then used with the market price as a ratio:

$$\frac{\text{Market price per share}}{\text{Earnings per share}}$$

Continuing with the same example:

A 50 pence share in ABC Petroleum Plc pays a dividend of 22 pence and its quoted price is 296 pence. The current dividend yield is 7.43%.

Profit for the year, after tax, was £1,800,000 and the number of shares issued is 7,000,000.

$$\text{P/E ratio} = \frac{296}{25.71}$$
$$= 11.51$$

Once again, this can be compared with other P/E ratios in peer group companies in the Oil sector. As with dividend yield, this is an assessment of past performance, but the market price, as we shall see, is very much a matter of investor expectations of future dividends. Certain institutions have very high P/E ratios; this is perhaps because in the eyes of the investor, these companies have very high future growth potential.

24.4   Dividend cover

Before moving on to the compound arithmetic of predicting future price on the strength of future dividend, it is appropriate to include a final ratio used by the stock market to assess performance. This is dividend cover. Once again it is a backward looking measure of performance.

This is calculated as follows:

$$\frac{\text{Earnings per share}}{\text{Dividend per share}}$$

A 50 pence share in ABC Petroleum Plc pays a dividend of 22 pence and its quoted price is 296 pence. The current dividend yield is 7.43%.

Profit for the year, after tax, was £1,800,000 and the number of shares issued is 7,000,000. EPS was 25.71 and the P/E ratio 11.51.

Therefore:

$$\frac{25.71}{22.00}$$
$$= 1.17$$

This figure represents the degree of reinvestment of earnings.

The yield of a share at any point is made up of price change since purchase, plus any dividend income. Unlike bonds, dividend income is not certain and by no means constant. Indeed, investors will often seek a larger dividend year after year, particularly if the price of the share is constantly rising too. Thus dividend yield is an important factor in driving the share price. It is by no means the only factor of course. For example, in terms of the common ratios given above, the amount of dividend cover is important for shareholders in that it indicates over a series of results, the degree of commitment that the company has to retain earnings for future investment, to provide better future returns for shareholders.

24.5 Evaluating share price and yield

The ratios we have looked at represent history. As a series, they can be used as an indicator of the trend of the company's performance. To take an investment decision we need to look at history of course, but equally we need to build in our expectations of future share performance.

Example

Initially we look back to an earlier example:

A 50 pence share in ABC Petroleum Plc purchased at 275 pence, paid a dividend of 22 pence and its quoted price is now 296 pence. The current dividend yield is 7.43%.

The simple yield over the last year can be calculated as follows:

$$\frac{(MP - PP + DV) \times 100}{PP}$$

where

MP = market price
PP = purchase price
DV = dividend

Substituting

$$\frac{(296 - 275 + 22) \times 100}{275}$$

$$= 15.64\%$$

This is a combination of capital growth and income, as a percentage of the original purchase price of the investment.

This is still only retrospective; that is you can calculate a historic yield. Investments, however, should also look forward. You buy an investment for what it is expected to yield. However, we can use this number as it represents the sort of yield we might expect for a particular type or class of share, in a particular industrial sector.

For the future, we should therefore substitute *expected* dividend, together with *expected* price growth (if any). This is the capitalisation rate. We can manipulate the formula above, given dividend forecast and also assuming the rate of growth is maintained. This will enable us to forecast price.

Example

A share, which normally yields some 15.64%, is forecast to grow from 275 pence and maintain its dividend of 22 pence. What price do we expect it to achieve?

$$(275 \times 1.1564) - 22 = 296$$

We have multiplied up the price by the expected yield and then stripped out the expected (maintained) dividend of 22 pence. This leaves us with the expected price.

Manipulating this we can also assess, using present value techniques, what price we would expect the share to trade at today, given a rate of yield comparable with other shares in the same risk class. This can then be compared with what it is actually trading at. This then takes us back to the question of NPV.

$$\text{Price today} = \frac{\text{Coupon} + \text{Expected price}}{1 + \text{Rate of yield for security}}$$

Using our earlier share information, its class should yield some 15.64% on average, the dividend forecast is 22 pence and the forecast for the share price is 296 pence.

Substituting

$$\text{Price today} = \frac{22 + 296}{1.1564}$$

$$= 275 \text{ pence}$$

If it is trading at a price below this figure, we have a positive NPV and the investment would seem to be worthwhile, on the assumptions made. In other words, on our data, the share is under-priced today.

The efficiency of the stock market in which the share is trading will drive the price to this "fair value". If the risk factor rises, due to economic changes in that particular industrial sector, the price will fall, as the yield rises. The coupon and future price are discounted at a greater yield:

$$\text{Price today} = \frac{22 + 296}{1.17}$$

$$= 271 \text{ pence}$$

Another arithmetic link might be demonstrated when the dividend forecast is downgraded. The price/yield relationship will change and the price will also fall. This link is derived from the fact that generally speaking, all investments of the same risk category will tend to yield the same.

We have, so far, only considered the yield calculations in a "simple" way. Shares, of course, are a perpetual security, with no redemption. This means that we should look further forward into the next and later years. For this we revert to the compound yield calculations we examined in earlier chapters.

Today's price was easily determined from dividend and price forecasts:

$$P^0 = \frac{D^1 + P^1}{1 + i}$$

where
P^0 = price today
D^1 = dividend at end of year 1
i = the yield for the class of security

We can calculate what the price is at P^1, by moving all the information one year further on:

$$P^1 = \frac{D^2 + P^2}{1 + i}$$

where
P^1 = price at the beginning of next year
D^2 = forecast dividend at end of year 2
P^2 = the forecast price at the end of year 2
i = the yield for the class of security

It follows that the Present Value of this sum can be calculated:

$$P^1 = \frac{D^2 + P^2}{(1 + i)^2}$$

Add to this the Present Value of the dividend at the end of year 1, which is:

$$\frac{D^1}{1 + i}$$

and we have the price of the share today, including forecast dividends for the next two years and the price at the end of year two.

$$\frac{D^1}{1 + i} + \frac{D^2 + P^2}{(1 + i)^2}$$

Using substituted figures, we have a share priced at 273. Is this good value, considering the yield for the sector is 13%, dividend forecasts are 20 pence in the first year and 25 in the second, when the expected price will be 300?

$$\frac{20}{1.13} + \frac{25 + 300}{1.13^2} = 17.69 + 254.52$$

$$= 272.21$$

We can conclude that a fair price for the share would be about 272 pence.

The formula we have used above can be extended indefinitely, using conventional compounded discounting. The rate used for the discounting of the cashflows is the capitalisation rate.

A point to note here is that since the arithmetic is identical to a bond paying different coupons, you could use the IRR and NPV function to calculate the yield of a share, given assumptions as to future price and dividend growth. Then, given assumptions on growth rate in the share price, NPV will tell you whether the price you have is good value or not.

25 Bonds with equity warrants

25.1 Introduction

A borrower of funds in capital markets has to compete for finite resources. This means that the more incentive an issuer can offer an investor, the better the chance that the required level of funding can be successfully attained.

At the same time, the borrower/issuer is painfully aware that an incentive which will allow his issue to be extremely successfully sold down, could cost him dear in high levels of yield.

Somewhere between the two, the successful capital market originator will be able to come to a compromise which enables an issue to be successful, but not unduly burdensome to the issuer.

These investor incentives can vary tremendously. We have already seen some types of innovation such as stepped coupon bonds, bonds with delayed coupons, and zeros all of which are variations on a theme which will appeal to certain types of investor with certain tax profiles.

An alternative variation of the simple "straight" (any fixed income bond) is the bond with warrants attached. These warrants allow the holder of the bond to purchase currency at a predetermined rate (currency warrants). Other bonds allow the purchase of gold at a predetermined rate and some allow the purchase of more of the same type of bonds, at a later issue.

The type to be considered here is the bond with equity warrants attached. These warrants allow the holder of the bond (should he wish) to subscribe to an issue of shares in the company issuing the bond. If the price set for "conversion" of the warrants (not to be confused with convertible bonds where the bond itself is exchanged for shares, gold, currency, more bonds etc.) is a good one in prospect, then the investing institutions will take up the issue and it will sell well. Alternatively, the warrants may be separated from the bonds and traded in their own right.

Warrants to buy are essentially call options on an underlying share, commodity or currency. As such they develop value like options, as the price of the underlying instrument rises. The main differences between warrants and ordinary stock options is that there is only one strike price available for exercise and there is only one expiry date, instead of several. Warrants may be available for baskets of shares also, rather than single shares; perhaps a basket may be founded on a specific industrial sector.

It is as well to note that in addition to judging the right price at which to issue the bond, the right price for the share and the right time and market conditions, the issuer and his originator must be aware of the effect on existing shareholders whose holdings will be subject to "dilution", i.e. there will be more shares in the company in the market over which the company's earnings must be spread and the consequent effect of this on the share price.

Bonds which are issued which result in the issue of new shares will cause dilution if the warrants are exercised. Other types of warrants are those which are exercisable into existing stock. Depending on whether an issuer has or has not got these shares in portfolio, the warrants will be said to be covered or uncovered. The exercise of such warrants will not cause dilution.

At this point we can have a look at some of the relevant calculations which are used in bonds with equity warrants, in a specific case. A currency play is quite common, particularly for yen bonds, so the example includes a US dollar/Swiss franc currency exchange.

Problem

Walter Schetzer S.A. raised SF250 million for 10 years with a bond issue with warrants attached paying an annual coupon of 4.50%. The bonds were issued at par.

The issue was as follows:

Bond denomination:	SF5,000,00 per bond
One warrant per bond:	150 shares per warrant at US$8.08 per share (US$1212.00 per warrant)
Exchange rate at issue:	US$/SF1.6500
Share price at issue:	US$6.67

For comparison purposes the alternative straight issue SF200 million would have been at a coupon level of 5.25%.

25.2 Conversion premium

The performance of the company's shares in the past has been good. With this in mind it has been decided to set the conversion price, or exercise price in option terminology, at $8.08 per share, compared with the current share price of $6.67. This means that if the company does well during the life of the issue, its share price will rise and the warrant can be exercised for profit when the share price rises and hopefully continues to rise above $8.08. At the moment, therefore, also in options terminology, the value of the warrant is entirely time value, because the strike price of what in effect is a call option on the shares, is above the current market price. The options are out-of-the-money.

Note: do not confuse conversion premium with the premium payable under an option. They are entirely different things.

The formula for calculating the conversion premium is:

$$CV = \frac{CP - SP}{SP} \times 100$$

where
SP = share price
CP = conversion price
CV = conversion premium

Substituting

$$\frac{8.08 - 6.67}{6.67} \times 100$$

$$= 21.14\%$$

Therefore the conversion price is at a premium of 21.14% to the current share price. This, in option terms, is the degree of difference between the strike rate and the current market rate, the option being out-of-the-money. Conversion premium will fall as the price of the share rises to the point where the exercise price of the warrant is the same as the share price in the market place. Should the stock market suffer a fall, then conversion premium will rise once again, perhaps to the point where it is so large that, even given considerable volatility in the share price, it will never be exercised. The warrants then expire worthless.

25.3   Warrant cost

Earlier in this chapter, we said that we would expect an ordinary straight bond issued by this borrower to carry a coupon of 5.25% p.a. The coupon of the issue is 4.50% compared with 5.25%. In other words if we ignore the incentive of the warrants for a moment, what would a 4.50% coupon bond be worth (in price) compared with an identical 5.25% bond? Clearly much less; but by how much?

Using the HP12C, calculate what the price of a straight bond would be, with a yield of 5.25%, and a coupon also of 5.25%. This would be par.

Key	Display	
FV	100	(par value of bond)
PMT	5.25	(coupon of issue)
i	5.25	(comparable yield of 10-year bonds)
n	10	(bond life)
PV = = = = >	− 100.00	

Having done this, change the coupon to the value in our issue with warrants of 4.50%.

Key	Display	
FV	100	(par value of bond)
PMT	4.50	(coupon of issue)
i	5.25	(comparable yield of 10-year bonds)
n	10	(bond life)
PV ??? = = = = >	−94.28	

Thus with a purchase price of 100% and the same value at redemption it is worth only 94.28% to the investor at time of issue. The value discount being 100 − 94.29 = 5.72% less. In other words, if the warrants were stripped off and the basic bond traded with a 4.50% coupon, it would trade at about 94.28.

A warrant cost per individual bond of 5.72% per SF5,000.00.

Looking at this in option terms, the issuer has written a call option to the investor, in exchange for a premium of 5.72 per cent, which gives the investor the right, but not the obligation, to buy shares at some time in the future (a European style option in fact), at an exercise price of US$8.08.

It is worth mentioning here that in recent times, bonds issued by certain Japanese borrowers, carrying warrants on the company's shares were considered so valuable in terms of the value of the warrants that the bonds carried a negative yield. In other words, the investor was prepared to lose money on the bond, because its coupon was so low, in exchange for the very valuable option to buy equity stock in the issuer, which was not otherwise obtainable.

Having already seen the cost of the warrants in terms of the reduced coupon and its effect on price, we now can consider the cost of the warrant in dollars. This takes into account the exchange rate play.

This is calculated as follows:

$$\frac{NV \times WC}{SW \times 100 \times ER}$$

where

NV = nominal value per bond
WC = percentage cost of warrant
SW = number of shares per warrant
ER = current exchange rate

WC and ER will vary depending on market conditions as comparative yields on bonds with similar maturities vary and exchange rates move.

Substituting

$$\frac{5,000.00 \times 5.72}{150 \times 100 \times 1.6500}$$

$$= US\$1.16$$

In other words, the dollar cost per share tells you what the cost of the warrants is to the investor, on the basis of a per share cost. This means that, in option terms again, the shares will actually cost $8.08 plus $1.16 in warrant cost which is like premium, making a total cost of $9.24. If yields on comparative bonds change, and the ex-warrant bond price rises from 94.28 to par, then the investor who purchased at issue at par is, in effect, holding a free warrant. Equally, if exchange rates move, and the Swiss franc falls in value to 1.6800 perhaps, then the US dollar cost will also fall as the dollar strengthens.

The exchange rate element is omitted for single currency transactions.

The dollar cost per share is $1.16 as we have seen. We can also measure this as a percentage of the share price:

$$\frac{1.16}{6.67} \times 100$$

$$= 17.39\%$$

which is 17.39% of the current share price.

We may note that, falling back on basic option theory, the higher the initial warrant cost (here stated as 5.72%, but however it is expressed), the greater must be the volatility of the underlying share price. Volatility of share price is among the most significant factors in option pricing. With high volatility, however, comes a greater chance of profitable exercise.

25.4   Warrant premium

Warrant premium is the combination of conversion premium as a percentage of share price and warrant cost also as a percentage of share price.

The investor is subject to the conversion premium at 21.14% and also the cost of the warrant by virtue of the fact that the value of the bond he pays 100% for is worth 94.28% or a percentage dollar cost per share of 17.39%.

A total warrant premium, taking all things into account, of 38.53%.

The factors that affect warrant premium, include the comparative yields of other bonds, exchange rates in this case, plus changes in the share price giving a greater or lesser conversion premium.

25.5   Gearing

A further important measure in warrant issues is their gearing. This is the ratio of current share price to the dollar cost of the warrant per share. Current share price is $6.67 at issue and the cost per share of the warrant is $1.16.

The formula below will provide us with the gearing number:

$$\frac{CP}{WC} = \text{gearing}$$

Substituting

$$\frac{6.67}{1.16} = 5.75$$

The gearing in this case is 5.75, but what does this mean?

In a stock option strategy, if we buy a call option, we are in a leveraged position. We pay a comparatively small premium, which gives us the opportunity to buy shares at an agreed price, at some time in the future.

For example we might pay 25 pence a share for a six-month option to buy a share at 300 pence when it is already trading at that level – an at-the-money call. If the price of the share rises, through 325 pence and beyond, our option will behave progressively more and more like the underlying share. What we have done is to gain access to a speculative play on the price of the share, but at a cost of just over 8 per cent of the value of the share. This is leverage or gearing. In this case, we can buy 12 times as many options on the shares at 25 pence as shares at 300 pence.

The investor with warrants is in the same sort of position. In order to buy shares, in the continuing example we have been looking at, he would have to spend 5.75 times as much, $6.67 for the share, instead of $1.16 for the warrant to buy the same share. This is warrant gearing.

25.6 Warrantability

A final measure which is encountered in bonds with equity warrants, is warrantability. This is the ratio of the value of the shares per warrant (at the conversion price), per bond. This example is complicated by the dollar/Swiss franc currency conversion.

Value of shares per warrant at conversion price =

$$150 \times 8.08 = US\$1212.00 \times 1.6500 = SF1999.80$$

$$\text{warrantability} = \frac{1999.80}{5000.00} \times 100$$

$$= 40.00\%$$

This is the value of the shares which the investor has the option of purchasing, at the exercise price of US$8.08 (SF13.33 equivalent) expressed as a percentage of the face value of the bond. High warrant-ability gives the investor the ability to convert a high percentage of the face value of the bond into shares.

General conclusion

These numbers represent a variety of ways in which a particular issue can be assessed as more or less attractive to investors. The numbers must therefore be used comparatively.

Typically an investor will ask such questions as, given the past perform-ance of the share, is the conversion premium too high?

Or perhaps, given the state of the (bond) market in warrant issues, which of course is intimately connected with the stock market on which the shares are quoted, is the warrant cost (that sacrifice and difference between what one would get by way of coupon for a non-warrant issue, compared with the coupon on the issue in question), too high? Buyers of stock options are put off in the same way by too high an option premium.

The investor is balancing what is being sacrificed by way of coupon, against the value of the option which is being written by the issuer, in the form of warrants. Some yen bonds actually achieved negative yields in the past, during bull runs on the Tokyo Stock Exchange. This is because the coupons were very low and the options to purchase shares were seen as such good value by investors. They were prepared to lose money on the bonds for the access to the shares.